Adult ESOL Learners in Britain

Multilingual Matters

The Age Factor in Second Language Acquisition
  D. SINGLETON and Z. LENGYEL (eds)
Approaches to Second Language Acquisition
  R. TOWELL and R. HAWKINS
Asian Teachers in British Schools
  PAUL A. S. GHUMAN
Child-Rearing in Ethnic Minorities
  J.S. DOSANJH and PAUL A.S. GHUMAN
Coping with Two Cultures
  PAUL A. S. GHUMAN
Encyclopedia of Bilingualism and Bilingual Education
  COLIN BAKER and SYLVIA PRYS JONES
Intercultural Communication
  ROBERT YOUNG
Language Planning: from Practice to Theory
  ROBERT B. KAPLAN and RICHARD B. BALDAUF, Jr
Language Policies in English-Dominant Countries
  MICHAEL HERRIMAN and BARBARA BURNABY (eds)
Literacy, Language and Community Publishing
  JANE MACE (ed.)
Mainstreaming ESL
  JOHN CLEGG (ed.)
Multicultural Child Care
  P. VEDDER, E. BOUWER and T. PELS
Quantifying Language
  PHIL SCHOLFIELD
Second Language Practice
  GEORGES DUQUETTE (ed.)
Working with Bilingual Children
  M.K. VERMA, K.P. CORRIGAN and S. FIRTH (eds)

Please contact us for the latest book information:
Multilingual Matters, Frankfurt Lodge, Clevedon Hall,
Victoria Road, Clevedon, BS21 7HH, England
http:/www.multi.demon.co.uk

Adult ESOL Learners in Britain: A Cross-Cultural Study

A.L. Khanna   Mahendra K. Verma

R.K. Agnihotri   S.K. Sinha

MULTILINGUAL MATTERS LTD
Clevedon • Philadelphia • Toronto • Sydney • Johannesburg

Library of Congress Cataloging in Publication Data

Adult ESOL Learners in Britain: A Cross-Cultural Study
A.L. Khanna [et al.]
Includes bibliographical references and index
1. English language–Study and teaching–Foreign speakers.
2. English language–Study and teaching–Great Britain.
3. Minorities–Great Britain–Education–Language arts.
I. Khanna, Amrit Lal.
PE1128.A2A328   1998
428'.007'041–dc21   97-47656

British Library Cataloguing in Publication Data

A CIP catalogue record for this book is available from the British Library.

ISBN 1-85359-335-4 (hbk)
ISBN 1-85359-334-6 (pbk)

Multilingual Matters Ltd

UK: Frankfurt Lodge, Clevedon Hall, Victoria Road, Clevedon BS21 7HH.
USA: 1900 Frost Road, Suite 101, Bristol, PA 19007, USA.
Canada: OISE, 712 Gordon Baker Road, Toronto, Ontario, Canada M2H 3R7.
Australia: P.O. Box 586, Artamon, NSW, Australia.
South Africa: PO Box 1080, Northcliffe 2115, Johannesburg, South Africa.

Typeset by Wayside Books, Clevedon.
Printed and bound in Great Britain by the Cromwell Press Ltd.

Contents

Acknowledgements

A project of this nature could not have been completed without the active collaboration of a large number of people and institutions. We are grateful to all those who have helped us in our research, though we alone should be held responsible for any errors that may follow.

We are particularly grateful to the following 13 ESOL centres for their help and cooperation: Shepherds Lane, Leeds; Burton Road, Leeds; Bolton Royd, Bradford; York College of Arts and Technology, York; Neighbourhood English Scheme, Preston Road, London; Camden Adult Education Centre, London; Bethnal Green Centre, Tower Hamlets Institute of Adult Education, London; Midland Road Centre, Walsall; Walsall College of Technology, Walsall; The Parade Community Education Centre, Cardiff; Wilkie House, Edinburgh; Wester Hailes Educational Centre for NET, Edinburgh; Toll Cross Community Centre, NET, Edinburgh.

Thanks are due to the students, teachers and coordinators of all the above ESOL centres. In particular, we would like to record our appreciation of the help of Jan Bartholomew, Flick Thorpe, Paula Gains, Pat Bryden, Abeda Laher, Adele Attwood, Anne Spiers, John Fitzpatrick, Zakia Butt, Helen Bishop, Nicky Palmer, Carol Morris, Nissar Ahmed, David Lively, Nancy Sprat, Munira, Angus Kean, John Roberts, Linda Dicks, Peter Peak, Linda Thompson, Narinder Singh, Philippa Leicester, Pat Green, Valerie Purcell and Saligram Shukla. Not least was the help of Sabine Gupta, Paul Mathiesen, Joan Weir, Celia Roberts, Ann Janssen, T. C. Jupp, Tuku Mukherjee, Susan Sun, Euan Reid and Inder Gera in taking part in very useful interviews and discussions. We are also grateful to Hong Lu, A. Mukherjee and Meghna for helping us with translating our English questionnaire into Chinese, Bengali and Urdu. Thanks are also due to C. Shekhar Verma, Dharam Pal, C. Pant, Ghalib, Neelam, Narendra Kaushik, Mike Grover and Usha Verma. We are grateful to all the ESOL teachers who attended the Inservice Teacher Training (INSET) Programmes at the University of York. We have constantly been receiving very constructive feedback from ESOL teachers and from the members of NATECLA. Thanks are also due to the Nuffield Foundation, UK, the British Council, New Delhi, and the Department of Language and Linguistic Science, University of York, for making this research possible.

Preface

As a consequence of several economic and political reasons there has been an enormous amount of migration to English-speaking countries such as Britain, Canada, America and Australia during the last four to five decades of this century. The migrants in their new environments felt the need to learn English to cope with the demands of their everyday lives and work more effectively towards their economic and social advancements. As these adult migrants already spoke another language and came from another geographical and cultural background, their learning of English raised several educational, linguistic, cultural, psychological, social and pedagogical issues which are of great concern to the second language researcher and pedagogue.

This book examines some of the social, psychological and linguistic aspects of learning English by bilingual adult migrants belonging to various cultural and geographical backgrounds; it is based on research carried out in 1989 in 13 adult education ESOL (English for Speakers of Other Languages) centres located in various parts of the UK. The research could not have been conducted without a Nuffield Foundation Travel Fellowship. Besides tracing a brief history of ESOL in Britain, the authors present a detailed profile of the ESOL learners' socio-economic, linguistic and cultural background. As well as analysing the migrants' attitudes and motivation towards English and their desire to maintain their mother tongues or heritage languages, the book describes how the ESOL teachers and supervisors design their curriculum, produce teaching materials and evolve the tools and procedures to evaluate the progress made by the learners. It also attempts to enumerate the variety of teaching strategies used in ESOL classes and highlights the strategies that the learners appreciate and are successful at using. It also stresses the teachers 'desire for' teacher training not only in various methodologies of teaching but also in developing a positive attitude towards the language and cultural background of the learners and using it as a rich resource for language teaching. In the interest of consistency (and except in actual citations), we have used the abbreviation ESOL (rather than ESL) throughout the book.

The book is intended for ESOL researchers, applied and sociolinguists and others who are interested in the issues relating to second language learning and teaching in a native language setting.

Abbreviations

(Only ESOL-related abbreviations included)

AEI	Adult Education Institute
ALBSU	Adult Literacy and Basic Skills Unit
DES	Department of Education and Science
ESL	English as a Second Language
ESOL	English for Speakers of Other Languages
ET	Employment Training
FE	Further Education
FEFC	Further Education Funding Council
HMI	Her/His Majesty's Inspector
ILEA	Inner London Education Authority
LEA	Local Education Authority
MSC	Manpower Service Commission
NATECLA	National Association of Teachers of English and Other Community Languages to Adults
NEC	Neighbourhood English Classes
NFER	National Foundation for Educational Research
NVQ	National Vocational Qualification
NATESLA	National Association of Teachers of English as a Second Language to Adults
TEC	Training and Enterprise Council
TOPS	Training Opportunities Scheme
TSAS	Training Standards Advisory Service
YTS	Youth Training Scheme
SLA	Second Language Acquisition

1 ESOL Learners in Britain: A Sociolinguistic and Historical Background

Introduction: Language and Imperialism

It would not be an exaggeration to suggest that the history of the Anglo-Saxons' ascendance to power, in Britain and overseas, has been a long and protracted chronicle of English linguistic and political colonisation. Politically it has been a history of imperialism and expansion. From a sociocultural perspective, it has been a subtle but deliberate process of attempted cultural assimilation. From a sociolinguistic point of view, it has involved the politically and economically powerful English-speaking group creating conditions in society, education and administration which have not only undermined the dominated communities' (colonised subjects, refugees, minorities, etc.) positive attitudes towards mother tongues but also promoted feelings of inadequacy about the mother tongues, and has thus contributed to the redistribution of these subverted mother tongues and English over new domains. Pedagogically, it has resulted in the imposition and relentless promotion of the English language, and the development of teaching of English as a Foreign Language (EFL), English as a Second Language (ESL) and English for Speakers of Other Languages (ESOL), making it post-imperial Great Britain's invaluable tool to wield global influence as well as a marketable asset. Addressing 'Britain in the World' Conference held in London on 29 March 1995, David Puttnam (an eminent British film director, now Lord Puttnam) advocated that private and public money should support the BBC World Service and the British Council in cornering the international education market. He then went on to add: 'We will never be the World's factory again, but we could be the World's University … One country will corner the market and it will be an English-language country. I want it to be us.' (*The Times*, 30 March 1995: 12)

According to Roger Bowers, Assistant Director-General, British Council, the 'English 2000' initiative launched by the Prince of Wales

> unashamedly seeks to promote British goods and services – the books and
> examinations, teaching and training, consultancy and research that add up

1

to a huge visible and invisible export business for the English language ...
we must encourage the view that if you want to learn English, you should
buy British. (*The Times*, 6 April 1995: 15)

It is apparent that the awareness of the distinction between EMT (English as
Mother Tongue), EFL and ESL did not hit the consciousness of the applied
linguists and the pedagogues until the beginning of the end of British colonialism
in the Asian and African subcontinents. This, however, does not mean that
pedagogic and political aspects of the teaching of English were not on the
agenda of the administrators and educationists. Although the Romans, the
Anglo-Saxons (including the Jutes), the Picts, the Scandinavians and the Normans,
one after the other, invaded Great Britain, and settled there, these contacts
did not give rise to grassroot bi/multilingualism. After a spell of Celtic–Latin
bilingualism and a longer period of English–French elite bilingualism, English
eventually prevailed, and in 1362 it became the official language of the court.
The rise and domination of the Standard English dialect in education, administration and industry, at the cost of the indigenous Celtic languages, continued
unabated.

This chapter is divided into four sections. The first section presents a brief
history of development of teaching English/ESOL to indigenous non-English
speakers and to non-English speaking non-indigenous arrivals in the UK since
the time when the Anglo-Saxons emerged as the dominant community in the
country. It traces the evolution of a succession of monolingual approaches of
teaching English to non-English speaking communities. The first section will
concentrate on the impact of the English language (invariably accepted as
superordinate, Verma, 1986, 1993) and English power, i.e. the power of the
Anglo-Saxons and their supporters on the indigenous Gaelic minorities in Wales,
Scotland and Ireland. In the second section we will examine the attitudes
and motivation of the first well-documented group of French-speaking Huguenot
refugees towards learning English within a bilingual paradigm. An attempt will
be made to highlight the socioeconomic discrimination which they confronted,
and how in the absence of any initiatives on the part of either the state or the
dominant English community to help them learn English and foster bilingualism,
the refugees had to pool their expertise and resources to achieve it. The third
section will discuss the language needs of the European refugees, including the
Jews, who arrived in the UK during the two world wars. The final section will
highlight how the need to provide cheap labour to post-World War II British
industries prompted the government to encourage immigration of these mainly
non-white workers from the colonies and the newly independent Commonwealth
countries, in particular the South Asian countries. These countries had suffered
socioeconomic destabilisation and exploitation as well as sociolinguistic inequity
and insecurity not only during the period they were colonised but also after they

had won political freedom. It looks at the attitude of the host community towards these new immigrants (who, irrespective of their skills and experience were placed on the lowest rung of the social hierarchical structure below the white working classes) and towards their language and culture; and how these contributed to the emergence and development of the concept of ESOL in the 'assimilative' mould. We will also examine the gradual changes in the aims and objectives of ESOL teaching – from enabling survival and promoting welfare to providing accredited courses as well as support on mainstream educational and vocational courses to enable bilinguals to attain their full potential and thereby make the promise of 'equal opportunities' an attainable possibility.

English Language in Wales, Scotland and Ireland

After the conquest and colonisation of England and the gradual annexation of the Celtic nations known now as Wales, Scotland and Ireland (including Northern Ireland), there was a period of monolingualism among the Welsh, Irish and Scottish masses, and elite bilingualism among the landed gentry and aristocracy led by the Royalty. Latin and Greek, the classical languages of education, administration and religion, dominated the British nations. The Norman French conquest of England introduced English–French bilingualism among the upper crust of society, including the Royalty, but English, which was initially considered inferior to classical languages, and which was perceived as a vulgar tongue in comparison with Latin and French, did not have to suffer this indignity for long. The growing feelings for the mother tongue and antipathy towards both Latin and French are clearly reflected in Poole (1646) who noticed how children were puzzled and confounded by being asked to parse Latin before they had the least knowledge of the mother tongue. According to Maittaire (1712), the children were forced to learn what they could not understand, and were hurried into Latin before they could read English. Joseph Aickin was, however, aware of the lack of appropriate vocabulary in English to cope with the demands made on it. Aickin (1693) felt strongly that all learning should take place through the mother tongue, i.e. English; but before this could happen, English, he argued, should become copious enough to express all ideas and emotions. It is obvious that in the process of the acceptance and adoption of English as the preferred language by the Norman conquerors themselves, as well as by the landed gentry and aristocracy, the concept of the mother tongue had begun to become synonymous with the English language. This rise of English and English consciousness among the Anglo-Saxons and their supporters also signalled the subordination of the indigenous Celtic mother tongues. Once English became the court language, and language teachers began to experiment with teaching English as mother tongue, the indigenous mother tongues – Welsh, Cornish, Irish (Gaelic) and Scottish (Gaelic) – began to be marginalised. The introduction of Acts and Statutes contributed to the suppression and linguistic marginalisation of the indigenous communities with Celtic mother tongues. The absence of a legally sanctioned national/official language did not, however, imply an official or national philosophical stance of 'freedom of the individual in language choice' as Cheshire (1991) clearly states:

> The Welsh language entitlement enshrined in the new National Curriculum for Wales has had to wait for four hundred years, and in the meantime the shift to English had been firmly established. (Cheshire, 1991: 14)

The induced shift to English was slow but certain. According to Bellin (1984: 449), of the various British languages spoken in places like Cornwall, Devon, the Lake District and Southern Western Scotland, Welsh in Wales has been the only survivor, and even there it is spoken by a minority. The imposition of English on the Welsh and the Cornish populations was followed by its introduction in Scotland where Gaelic, and later Scots, had been thriving languages. Scots, after enjoying a period of prestige and power, was overrun by the supremacy of standard English, a language/dialect, the Scottish aristocrats had embraced as part of their new identity. As Aitken (1981: 72–90) has shown, the nonentity of Scots follows from its past history ... reflected in the Union of the Crowns in 1603 and of the Parliaments in 1707. The RP variety of standard English remains the national and official language of Scotland.

> ... associated with the 'civilized' Lowland population, and Gaelic with the savage Highlanders ... English pressed in from the top of the social hierarchy and spread steadily downward; until Gaelic moved from majority to minority language status. (Dorian, 1981: 53; Fasold, 1984: 222)

> As long as the fisher folk remained members of a distinct sociocultural group with Gaelic as its linguistic symbol, the language would continue to be learned and used. But since the fisherfolk were thought of and indeed, thought of themselves as a less worthy group of people, the moment social mobility became possible, the group would dissolve itself and its linguistic symbol would be abandoned in the process. (Fasold, 1984: 224)

In her in-depth study of this Gaelic community on which Fasold's description mentioned above is based, Dorian succinctly paints the new attitude of the community:

> ... individuals as fishers, there was a tendency to abandon Gaelic along with other fisher behaviours. As the same woman said: I think, myself, as the children from Lower Brora got older, they ... were ashamed to speak Gaelic, in case they would be classed as a – a fisher. (Dorian, 1981: 67)

The growing power and prestige of English, which started in the seventeenth century, has continued unabated and so has the process of its colonisation of the minds and the habitats of communities in countries as near as the Celtic nations of Scotland, Wales and Ireland and as far as the Third World countries of Asia, Africa and Latin America. Billy Kay, talking about the imposition of English on the Scots, quotes Carlyle: 'to every man bred in Scotland, the English language was in some respects a foreign tongue' (Kay, 1986: 94).

The Scottish Education Act of 1872 insisted on the use of English by teachers and pupils in the classroom:

> Now English as a spoken language was to be actively encouraged, and the children's Scots, presumably, actively discouraged. This was the beginning of education appearing as an alien imposition to many Scots, as their home language was systematically devalued and banned from school. (Kay, 1986: 114)

The shift to English in Wales, Scotland and Ireland appears to be irreversible. Pedagogically speaking it is a curious act of history that those who study Irish in the school curriculum today do it as a second language. This is in sharp contrast to the position of Irish in the constitution as a national and the first official language. The position of English in the constitution, however, is that of a second language when in actual fact it is the mother tongue of the vast majority, and is taught as a mother tongue!

This brief survey of the once Celtic Britain clearly shows how the use of English as the mother tongue was extended to and eventually accepted by non-English Gaelic speakers as the mother tongue. It is important to note, however, that there was no recognition of bilingualism of such speakers in education and the curriculum and there was no distinct methodology for the teaching of English as a second language, nor was there any programme for fostering and/or sustaining the new bilingualism that was potentially there.

The First Refugees: The Huguenots in Britain

The first sociolinguistic encounter the English had with foreigners was with the Huguenots, the French-speaking Protestant refugees. Although these highly skilled and educated professionals and craftsmen were warmly welcomed by Queen Elizabeth and the educated, well-established sections of the community, they had to face not only inequity and discrimination at the hands of the guilds, apprentices, and small business men but also petty indignities and even violence in their interaction with the host community. Sadly, one must add that this has been the lot of the under-privileged, including the immigrants, both white and black, through the ages and throughout the world. Describing the world the Huguenots had to live in, Howatt writes:

> Local grassroots hostility to foreigners could break out at any time. With both the most powerful nations of Europe, France and Spain, ranged

against them, the English were suspicious and jumpy. Rumours of foreign spies, Catholic agents, and conspiracies of every kind were flying about and small incidents frequently flared into ugly scenes in the overcrowded streets. The women and the elderly in particular would have been exposed to insults, if not outright physical danger, and a knowledge of everyday English was some protection against mindless scare-mongering. (Howatt, 1984: 14)

Such a situation today would call for national/state language planning as a part of the educational planning to cater for the linguistic needs of these non-English speakers, but these would be alien to Elizabethan England and as such there was neither an awareness nor an acknowledgement of these needs. The Huguenots had little choice but to fend for themselves and manage their learning and acquisition of English, including the strategies and methodologies involved therein. However, as Howatt (1984: 14) points out, literacy skills that were necessary for skilled craftsmen could not be acquired informally. There was no Adult Literacy and Basic Skills Unit (ALBSU) to meet the challenge of English illiteracy among the Huguenots as there is today to meet the needs of mono-lingual English illiterates, and, only by default, to meet the ESOL needs of the new non-English speaking, predominantly black bilingual immigrants and their children. The educated pedagogues among the Huguenots soon responded to the needs of their community, i.e. to help them develop proficiency in English, and maintain their mother tongue competence in French. The approach they adopted could be said to have laid the foundation of what later has been characterised as a version of the Bilingual Methods.

> The two small English manuals that Jacques Bellot wrote for the French-speaking refugees in the 1580s reflect these priorities of basic literacy and everyday conversation quite closely ... Bellot's *Schoolmaster* is a curious little book in many ways.... It starts with a fairly detailed account of the English alphabet and pronunciation, necessary information for those who had picked the language up informally and needed help with reading and writing.... We cannot blame Bellot for the inadequacy of these grammar notes considering that the English had so far failed to produce anything substantial themselves. (Howatt, 1984: 14–16)

In the Preface to his second book, *Familiar Dialogues* (1586) Bellot offers a sort of sociolinguistic apology for writing the text book.

> The experience having in the old time learned unto me what sorrow is for them that the refugiate in a strange country, when they cannot understand the language of that place in which they be exiled, and when they cannot make them to be understood by speech to the inhabitors of that country wherein they be retired ... I thought good to put into their hands certain

short dialogues in French and English. (Bellot, 1586, quoted in Howatt, 1984: 16)

Bellot's approach to the sections of 'topics' and 'situation' for his textbook was pragmatic, and gives the impression of being the precursor of modern day 'needs analysis' approach, and situation based textbooks. The topics typically include 'shopping', 'greeting', 'extending invitation', etc. It is interesting to note that while Bellot and his contemporaries were primarily concerned with foreign language teaching, one could not be quite sure that their approach to teaching EFL, using bilingual, situational-driven text-books was not intended to help the learners maintain and sustain their competence in their mother tongue, French as well. In spite of the simmering resentment of the native-born teachers, the refugee teachers had established a tradition of 'High standards for the teaching of languages in England' (Howatt, 1984), in particular the teaching of EFL. That the concept of ESOL did not emerge may be attributed to the fact that very few of these foreigners were initially granted letter of denization (citizenship rights) and as such these textbook writers did not anticipate their compatriots would settle down in Britain for ever. However, a large number of the Huguenots did eventually become British citizens. In order to preserve their bilingual and bicultural identity they set up their own churches and voluntary mother tongue classes. The pressures from the English, and the successes they could and did attain through English, however, proved too great to maintain French, and the shift to English was inevitable, as in the case of the Celts described earlier.

The Newer Minorities

The refugee problem

During and following the two world wars, a large number of refugees from the East European countries – the Poles, the Ukrainians, the Hungarians, the Lithuanians and others – came to Britain. In the 1930s for the first time the British establishment introduced programmes for teaching English to Jews and non-Jews at several of London's evening Adult Education Institutes (AEIs). The Polish Resettlement Act of 1947 resulted in assimilation and integration-driven programmes for teaching English to the Poles. The arrival of the Hungarians and others in the 1950s and 1960s resulted in the first visible sign of awareness of the need to adopt a different pedagogical approach. The local colleges began to introduce classes to cater for their English language needs via 'formal' English teaching lessons. Hendon Technical college, for example, had a course on English for foreigners. The ethos based distinction between 'the natives' and 'the foreigners', which had emerged during the Huguenots' efforts to learn English, was applied to these refugees, too, and they were placed in a similar pedagogical framework of language teaching. The anomaly in 'refugees' being treated as 'foreigners' rather than 'newcomers' or 'new citizens' was duly noted in sociological and linguistic observations. Williams (1958: 116) commented that they were here through no wish of their own and were learning the language out of necessity.

This appears to be a period of consolidation and further development of the concept of EFL originally developed by the French Huguenot tutors. However, there was a significant change in the socio-psychological context in which the two refugee groups had arrived, for while some of the Huguenots would not conceive of settling down in Britain and did eventually return, and others could not do so because they had been granted only a temporary right to stay, these East European refugees and their hosts knew they were here to stay and the attitude of the host community was to help them assimilate culturally and linguistically. The educationists, nevertheless, failed to realise that the Modern Foreign Language methodology and curriculum, which had traditionally been applied to successful classical language teaching, and could be extended to teaching English to the Huguenots, may not be appropriate for these new refugees. Nor did they make any effort to help the refugees maintain their heritage mother tongue. The refugees had, therefore, to set up their own voluntary mother tongue teaching classes for the preservation of their heritage and culture. Some of these classes have survived in cities even today, e.g. the Polish school in Bradford. On the whole, teaching these refugees English, mostly provided by volunteers and voluntary organisations, was at best *ad hoc* and hardly an organised activity. Few cities smaller than London and Birmingham had any EFL classes. The epithets of 'strangers' and 'foreigners' which were used to differentiate the Huguenots from the indigenous people, were now being applied to these refugees too and consequently discrimination against and distaste towards them continued to be the mode of English attitudes.

Immigrants from the Commonwealth and other parts of the world

The 1940s witnessed both the end of World War II and the beginning of dismantling of the British Raj in South Asia, East Africa and the West Indies. Unlike the 'religious' (the Huguenots) and 'political' (the East European) refugees, the immigrants from these countries were alleged to have come to Britain of their own volition for economic betterment. Their own perception of this migration and the chain migration that followed is, however, different. They feel that the economic disadvantage affecting these newly independent countries was the direct result of the long-term colonisation of these nations and their natives and the exploitation of their resources for the benefit of Britain. The prosperity of Britain was thus, undeniably linked with the socioeconomic, sociocultural and linguistic exploitation of these communities. In this respect the migration was a logical consequence of this process. In actual fact, some communities which were transplanted as 'indentured labourers' outside their country, held British passports (the East African Asians), and felt they had legitimate rights to migrate to Britain to avoid political and economic upheavals generated by emerging local indigenous nationalism. It is interesting to note that while the arrival of the religious or political refugees was perceived to have created 'refugee problems', these new arrivals were characterised by the state and the host community as 'immigrant problems'; problems they were nevertheless!

In economic terms these new immigrants were induced to come here to provide cheap labour that Britain required for the post-war economic building of the country. In terms of social attitudes the feelings of 'racism', prejudice' and 'discrimination' that they have had to face were not *so* very different from those that the Huguenots or the East Europeans had to contend with. In political terms they were, however, perceived as 'problems' because they were largely black. Given the fact that school education has been made compulsory and the state had begun providing the community with not only 'cradle to grave welfare' but also with 'education for life', the educational establishment could not remain indifferent to these new immigrants and their needs as they had been to that of the Huguenots. However, the educationists' response to the language needs of these immigrants, many holding British passport, was largely *ad hoc*, uneven and predictably an ethnocentric one. It adopted a monolingual approach, which may partially be held responsible for the fact that at educational institutions, especially schools, non-white children came to be perceived as 'problems'.

Language, Colour and Citizenship: The British Way of Life

The 1950s and 1960s were periods of intense, but *ad hoc* and disparate, localised activities so far as the language education of the immigrants was concerned. A large number of these activities were first started and located in London, which has traditionally attracted refugees and immigrants and where large numbers of these non-white new Commonwealth immigrants were settled. Birmingham, the second largest city, set up evening classes suitably called 'English for our coloured citizens'. Even though these classes were meant for these new citizens, it may be noted, the EFL teaching approach and methodology continued to dominate and, in attitudinal terms, the term 'migrant' was as negative as 'foreigner' had been. Besides, these initiatives continued to be based on the belief that assimilation, and for that matter accelerated assimilation, was the best way to tackle the problem, which had so far characterised the English Establishment's perception of their encounter with non-English speaking groups and their response to these groups. Accordingly, it was claimed that all that the immigrants needed to learn was *the English way of life*. Consequently, instead of helping the immigrants acquire/develop English language skills to enable them access to the services provided by private and public agencies/institutions not only to survive on the fringes but also to improve their education/training and thereby their ability to contribute to the community/country they lived in as well as their own socioeconomic well being, these ESOL teaching programmes were, for all intents and purposes, set up

> to introduce and expatiate on aspects of our national and civic life, for these men were now members of the community and should possess the *cultural qualifications of responsible citizens.* (Mayell, 1958: 273, our emphasis)

One hardly needs to point out that the goal of such ESOL teaching programmes was to anglicise these immigrants; to help them dispossess themselves of their linguistic and cultural heritage and acquire, instead, new sets of norms and values, rights and responsibilities as British citizens/residents. Despite the fond and fervent claims of its proponents, which incidentally won them Section XI funding for ESOL teaching in 1966, such ESOL teaching could not be the panacea to solve the 'immigrant problem', and thereby avoid, or at least contain, any future racial conflict, because it was ill conceived, had ignored certain basic facts and failed to address itself to the immigrants' problems. It failed to take into account, for example, that unlike the European refugees of the two world wars, these 'economic betterment'-seeking new Commonwealth immigrants, fondly hoping to return home eventually, were visibly – racially, culturally, etc. – so very different from the host community, and the legacy of the 'empire' – the myths and memories of events on which it had been founded and sustained, and the mutual distrust and prejudice that had built up during it – stood between the two communities often living as neighbours. Besides, not only did the bureaucracy responsible for organising such courses make little effort to publicise them among the target group, and schedule them at locations and times which would enable the immigrants to join the courses, but also such courses had little to nothing in them which could directly help the immigrants to ameliorate their sad plight and acquire the skills to enable them to improve their lot. It was not surprising, therefore, that these early ESL teaching programmes failed to reach most of the target groups and had very little impact on them or their position in the adopted country.

The immigrants were seriously handicapped by their inability to speak English. Their plight – of the men commuting between home and work, often on shifts and at unsocial hours, to survive and of their women folk confined within the ethnic ghettoes – however, did not remain unnoticed for long. It evoked appropriate response from volunteers representing the liberal strand in the British social fabric. In north-west London, it was Ruth Hayman who recognised that action was needed, and it was mainly due to her efforts that in 1970 Neighbourhood English Classes (NEC) were launched with four guiding principles:

1. It was not to be a charity but a professional service. Teaching must be done by qualified teachers who were paid for their work. Students must pay fees – even if only a nominal amount.
2. Classes must be small, informal, and at a familiar place in the neighbourhood ... students should not have more than 8–10 minutes walk between home and class.
3. They would cater specially for women ... the most neglected sections of the newer communities; men learned English at work, children at school, but housebound women were apparently not being reached.
4. The classes would teach everyday functional English to enable the women to make use of the amenities available in their neighbourhood, and to give them the means of relating to daily life in this country.

(Grant, 1993, in *NATECLA News* 41:7)

It was their (volunteers, mostly middle-class women like Ruth Hayman) concern for these largely rural, non-English speaking and often illiterate in their own mother tongue, immigrants and their determination to do something to help them which completely transformed the entire ethos of ESOL teaching – from being provided by a bureaucracy indifferent to the immigrants' lot. The volunteers were deeply concerned to promote the well-being of these immigrants, to anglicise and assimilate them, and they went out into the community to recruit students for the voluntary classes they had set up. According to Sheth (1984: 52–7) an almost door-to-door search for immigrant students started. Inspired groups of volunteers went around the streets in the pouring rain, canvassing for prospective students (Hallgarten & Hayman, 1984: 15).

Recalling the old times, an ESOL teacher characterised the recruitment drive as 'cold' canvassing. She spent many days visiting over 100 homes, personally explaining the need and advantages of the immigrants' joining English classes. According to Sheth (1984), initially the teachers experienced numerous hurdles in persuading immigrant women to join the neighbourhood classes: one had to struggle hard to change attitudes. The pressures to recruit sometimes resulted in approaches which in retrospect, appear to be hardly professional. According to Hallgarten & Hayman:

The day classes are attended by mothers who often come accompanied by their pre-school children. Although creche or other facilities are provided to cope with these babies, they are usually very much in attendance – under foot, on the chairs or tables, being fed, changed, taken to the loo, scolded and what have you. Lessons are conducted over and above, in spite of and sometimes with the unconscious collaboration of these offsprings. (Hallgarten & Hayman, 1984: 12)

However, it was not long before these teachers had acquired the expertise of a multi-media sales promotion in preparing the campaign brief for marketing their

ESOL course, focusing on the various ways/fields which would enable them to improve the quality of life for the immigrants in this country. Indu Sheth, one of the few bilingual ESOL volunteer teachers, working alongside her English colleagues gives a very clear account of the ESOL teachers' campaign brief, which we quote:

> *ESOL teachers campaign brief: marketing ESOL at no cost to the customers: a poster in a local library and a knock on the door.*
>
> Often the ESOL teachers prepared a written brief, which offered them guidelines how to sell their product to the newly arrived non-English speaking immigrants, specially women, The gist of the brief was to convince prospective students that if they had some knowledge of English, they would be better able to understand and appreciate the laws of this country and their own civil rights and responsibilities. In addition, they would be able to discuss their children's progress with the teachers when they visited their children's schools. They would learn enough to explain their physical ailments to their doctors, and in case of emergency they would be able to call an ambulance or the police. It would help them with their shopping, at the post office, and in the use of public transport. (Sheth, 1984: 54)

These marketing briefs, despite using capitalistic terms like 'product' and 'sell', highlight the pragmatic benefits and are indicative of these volunteers' acute empathetic perception of the problems faced by the immigrants, not only because they could not speak English but also because they had no access to the information/services which could make things easier for them. Recalling the difficulties her mother had to face, an ESOL learner who later became an ESOL teacher says:

> Finding work was not the only problem she had to overcome, she also had to learn how to cope with the local community. For instance, she was not aware that she could claim family allowance, put her name down for a council place, etc., which, if she had known, would have made life a little easier raising two young children. Watching mother struggle (not necessarily understanding only) was sad and hard but an invaluable experience which will always be with me. (Banarse, 1984: 59)

The NEC organisers were willing not only to listen to the personal problems of the potential ESOL learners but also to provide the classes to suit their needs and convenience. The teacher's will to help the newcomers was so strong that the potential ESOL learners' personal difficulties were readily recognised and responded to by the Neighbourhood English Classes (NEC). The first two classes started by NEC were day classes. Because many women had to go to work during the day, most neighbourhood classes were held in the evening. According to another teacher, the teaching/learning situation was, to say the least, rather difficult. These classes had very limited infrastructural facilities and it was often very difficult for the teacher to cope with the noise the students made in the class. According to Grant & Self (1984) there were in London: (a) six part-time classes for job seekers; (b) 22 day-time and two evening community classes; (c) one class for mentally handicapped adults in a local Adult Training Centre; (d) one class for physically handicapped adults; (e) one 21 hours per week foundation course for 12 students; and (f) two preparatory TOPS courses for 32 students. In addition, there were ESOL classes advertised as: (g) English for Pregnancy; (h) Link-skilled ESOL classes; (i) ESOL/Literacy – classes in cooking and English language, and sewing and English language; (j) '*Milan* clubs' (literally social get-togethers) for mothers and toddlers; (k) 'Beating the Language Barrier' – a course devised to help workers in health service communicate more effectively with patients with little or no English; and (l) the BBC '*Parosi*' (literally neighbour) new English language teaching programme. Initiatives that actually preceded the above programmes included Longman's Scope Series for young adults by Hadi and others, Industrial Language Training, by Jupp and Hodlin, etc. However, it was during the second half of the 1970s that there was considerable ESOL activity. The BBC soap opera *Parosi* encouraged some Asian women to learn English either through home-tuition or through formal ESOL classes. As Nicholls & Hoadley-Maidment (1988: 5) point out, many local education authorities, anticipating requests for guidance from a large number of non-English speaking immigrants, followed the BBC Adult Literacy Series *On the Move* and started making their own local contingency plans. The 1970s explored the issues concerning cross-cultural awareness. As Nicholls & Hoadley-Maidment write:

> The seventies closed with the second BBC series designed for bilingual adults, *Speak for Yourself* and the accompanying radio programmes for teachers of ESL. This series not only focussed on the language and access information required for day-to-day situations but also explored the issues of cross-cultural awareness, underlining the fact that communication is a two-way process with the onus for effective communication lying with non-native and native speaker of English alike. This refinement reflected the changing focus of the ESL curriculum at the time. (Nicholls & Hoadley-Maidment, 1988: 6)

The 'welfare' and 'missionary' roles that the ESOL teachers offered to play gradually drove them into pastoral work, listening to ESOL learners' personal and domestic problems and acting as unwilling counsellors. In spite of recent professionalism and the mainstreaming of ESOL, this attitude and role continues to prosper. The racism and inequality that the immigrants have had to experience have put them in a situation in which there has been an inevitable, but automatic forging of a bond between the learners and the largely white tutors. This was cemented by the introduction of the innovative 'Home Tuition schemes' which meant a tutor visiting their tutee in their home to offer one-to-one ESOL teaching. On many occasions learning/teaching English was prefaced by traditional minority culture based hospitality and sometimes even followed by culinary courtesies. This is in the age-old tradition of 'guru' (teacher) 'shishya' (pupil) relationship, which has not been dented by the personal linguistic, cultural and economic sufferings of the immigrants.

There has in recent years been a formidable alternative interpretation of the ESOL scenario of the 1960s and 1970s. The critics of the 'welfare' approach have claimed that in essence it was supporting the state in its ethnocentric and assimilationist policies, and the ESOL curriculum (unwritten in most cases) was not contributing to the linguistic development, and educational advancement of the ESOL adult learners. ESOL tutors as 'welfare' officers offering English for 'survival' became the general image. Although coaching in coping strategies was a laudable aim, it was rather restrictive, non-productive and short-sighted. Bhanot & Alibhai (1988) succinctly summarise the picture of 'a typical ESOL family' that emerges from an examination of some ESOL materials:

> The first thing that strikes the objective observer is that its members are appallingly accident-prone. They are constantly burning, scalding and cutting themselves or falling off ladders. In spite of strong warnings about throwing lighted matches into waste-paper baskets, they have managed to set their house on fire. This is probably a blessing in disguise, as the sink, basin, bath and loo were permanently blocked, the roof leaked and the kitchen ceiling had collapsed. They appear to be unhealthy. They are always telephoning the doctor and collecting prescriptions, but to little purpose, as once they get the medicine bottles home, they cannot get the tops off … Their conversation is limited to describing problems, complaining, apologizing and occasionally asking the way.

> There are some things they never do: argue, express opinions, go to meetings, study, laugh, tell stories, protest, run their own business. After unblocking all their loos, they don't have the energy. (Bhanot & Alibhai, 1988: 30)

According to Bhanot & Alibhai (1988) this sort of curriculum reflects the reality in a black family, or for that matter a white Italian or Cypriot Greek family. The stereotypical view of minority women as 'silent women' whose lack of control over English directly affects this acculturation process in embracing the 'British way of life', is part of the negative perception of many white ESOL tutors.

> There seems to be an underlying implication that no one can participate in real life unless they are fluent speakers of English … socializing with people who don't speak English is not socializing. (Bhanot & Alibhai, 1988: 32–3)

The lack of awareness and understanding of what 'real life' could mean to a multilingual was very real. They failed to appreciate that 'real life' meant several lives – cultural and linguistic and bilingual discourse did not have to be dependent on the acquisition and use of English. The argument in favour of a full curriculum has been gaining momentum since the mid-1980s. According to Janssen:

> I shall argue that success and achievement in education and training of bilingual learners must be underpinned by the acceptance of the principle of 'mainstreaming' – and access to the full curriculum on the basis of ability and potential. (Janssen, 1992: 66)

In small measures the new commitments and arguments of ESOL providers began to surface. In her interview with Jean McAllister, Anne Spiers (1992) describes some of these changes:

> We were part of a whole field that was changing ... As field ESOL teachers, we were beginning to realise that we shouldn't perpetuate a deficit model, and that we should challenge the curriculum as a whole, and how the institution operated.... One thing we have tried to do at Shipley is to encourage the institution and staff within it to see ESOL as part of language development, which is a mainstream issue for everybody, and also see ESOL as one part of the race-equality policy, which is an institutional commitment and a personal commitment for everybody. I think it is important for ESOL teachers to see that they are working in a social and economic and political context, and they have got a responsibility to have some perspective on that context. (Spiers, 1992: 12–13)

This change in attitudes toward ESOL objectives and ESOL learners was propelled by the opposition and resistance to monolingual and ethnocentric ethos embedded in lessons on 'the English way of life'. Both the learners and the bilingual and some monolingual tutors argued for pluralism, which meant cross-fertilisation of experiences through English and heritage languages.

> As part of our developing awareness of good practice and anti-racist teaching, many of us are already encouraging our students to write about their experiences and opinions in their own languages as well as in English. (*ILEA Newsletter,* 3 1984: 5)

During the 1970s and 1980s black tutors and other activists claimed that the move from the 'welfare-based' deficit model, which devalued learners' mother tongue, to 'bilingualism' had a continuing hidden agenda of racism. Kanji (1984), Mukherjee (1986), and others, advocated an 'anti-racist' model for ESOL. Mukherjee's (1986) 'ESL: An imported new empire?' echoed the radical strand in the debate. The impact of this on the pedagogical approaches was salient – the change in emphasis from monolingualism to pluralism and anti-racism was reflected in the change from EFL-based Direct Methods to situational–communicative, and bilingual methods. The role of the bilingual ESOL tutor also become more focused. As Nicholls & Hoadley-Maidment (1988) point out, by the late 1970s and early the 1980s, the belief in integration was beginning to be replaced by the reality of cultural pluralism.

ESOL, Language Support, the Market Forces and the 1990s

The acronym ESL began to be replaced by ESOL as a result of the black and white activists' arguments in favour of the teaching of English to adults within a multicultural and pluralist framework. The new ethos demanded an unequivocal acknowledgement of the prior experience – cognitive, linguistic and cultural that the ESOL learners brought to the classes. This change in approach and attitude is reflected in Thorpe (1994):

> It is vital, first and foremost, to define ESOL in this paper. The acronym has gained wide use as an umbrella term for teaching and learning of 'English as a Second or Foreign Language to Speakers of Other Languages' or 'English as a Second or Other Language'. Whereas the latter highlights the fact that for many learners English may indeed be a third or fourth language, the former is more commonly used. (Thorpe, 1994: 1)

The Education Reform Act (1988) was an attempt to shake up the educational system from primary schools to Further and Higher Education in England and Wales, and parallel developments have taken place in other parts of Britain. Adult and Further Education have not escaped the philosophy of 'market-forces', demanding among other things, 'self financing' courses and 'accountability' in terms of well-defined 'access' and 'progression' routes, as well as 'accreditation goals'. In the process of the restructuring and organising of this sector of education ESOL, fortunately, was not left out. The move towards mainstreaming and planning of courses based on 'needs' analysis and a negotiated curriculum got a fillip from the new government policy in the areas of education, training and unemployment. The emergence of the Further Education colleges from LEAs' control resulted in the inclusion of ESOL as a subject linked with various vocational skills on the one hand, and in accountability and professionalism on the other.

> The New Training Initiative launched in 1981 provided those 'progressives' with a desire to widen opportunities and curriculum in the F.E. sector with a chance.... For ESOL teachers seeking ways to get their students into mainstream classes this was a golden opportunity. ESOL practitioners were at the time exploring a methodology which involved analysing linguistically what happened in the classroom. This required that the ESOL teachers

accompany their students in the 'subject' lessons, observe, make notes, and then use that material for a language follow-up lesson which was delivered at another time in the week. This methodology was concerned with promoting the concept of partnership teaching. (Janssen, 1992: 85)

In Scotland this concept of partnership has been an important feature of vocational education and training since 1990, and has had its implications for ESOL teaching and learning. Mills believes that:

The relative non-marginalisation of the ESOL tutors, and to some extent the 'empowerment' of the ESOL learners at least began to be an integral part of the new approach. (Mills, 1994: 13)

It was this official demand for integration that provided the ESOL teachers with a legitimate base from which to demand full participation in curriculum development and the hope of achieving 'the partnership'.

Course profiles produced by ESOL teachers were positive information handed to subject teachers. These could not be ignored. The information provided could be used in the assessment and counselling parts of training programmes.... They gave subject teachers information about the skills bilingual learners might have as a result of previous educational or work experience. (Janssen, 1992: 87)

The HMI report (DES, 1992) adequately and clearly reinforces the fundamental factors which could contribute to bilingual ESOL adult's success. According to this report, 'bilingual adults achieve considerable success whenever a wide range of educational opportunities are open to them; certified provision incorporating language support is an effective response to their needs, as are courses leading to employment for which bilingualism is a prerequisite. Planning for progression, good initial guidance, counselling and assessment and recording of learning are fundamental to success'.

Since the mid-1980s several initiatives, e.g. YTS (Youth Training Scheme) and ET (Employment Training) have, it is claimed, offered more opportunities to both the tutors and the learners. But this has not been a panacea to bilingual pupils' needs and requirements. The Training Standards Advisory Service (TSAS) inspectors of the Employment Department, in their monitoring of the quality of training offered to ESOL learners (1991), did not give their stamp of approval. Ann Janssen quotes TSAS:

Many training providers in London have little or no understanding about the concept of ESOL with an occupational focus, and the need for language support for trainees from ethnic minority groups, with moderate language difficulties, who are working towards national vocational qualifications (NVQs). (Janssen, 1992: 104).

Ann Janssen, in her perceptive analysis of the situation with special reference to the contribution of the employers to the lack of success achieved by black ESOL trainees, says:

> Many providers foresaw a way of increasing their trainee numbers, and consequently their funding by recruiting bilingual trainees. However, few of the providers appreciated the necessary organisational changes that are required to meet the particular training needs of such learners. In fact many providers interpreted this funding as extra money being available to meet across the board costs, rather than enhancing what should already be an established quality standard to benefit their bilingual trainees. There was not the commitment to take on board the issues as would be described in a language policy. (Janssen, 1992: 112)

> The TP4 programme had a higher level of success with white trainees (i.e. East Europe refugees) on work placements than with black trainees (i.e. refugees from African origin) which gives us a possible indication of racist attitudes of employees. (Janssen, 1992: 113)

Sociological

The English colonisation of indigenous populations and the English reception of refugees and immigrants has been a continual story of racism, discrimination, inequality and exploitation – both linguistic and economic. The difference between the native whites' discrimination against the Huguenots, on the one hand, and the new Asian and African immigrants on the other, is that the latter, because of the colour of their skin, have had more of it. The Europeans too had their fair share of discrimination, though.

Linguistic

The influence of English has been so powerful and pervasive and its imperial role so widespread that it has always been assumed that within the language curriculum there is no room for two mother tongues. In other words, bilingualism cannot flourish under the shadow of or in association with English. Languages other than English have had inevitably to be placed in the Modern Foreign Language curriculum. The recent recognition of Welsh in Wales and the muted recognition of Gaelic in Scotland are examples of reluctant converts.

EMT, EFL, ES(O)L and language support

Our survey has clearly demonstrated that the late arrival of the conceptual framework of ESL and ESOL in the pedagogical world of applied English Linguistics is unambiguously associated with immigrant learners of English and their colonial past. It also smacks of the conflict between 'withdrawal' or 'marginalising' and 'mainstreaming', between ESL and EMT and between the desired ethos to assimilate the non-native and the lack of will to absorb them as 'English'. The teaching and learning of ESOL in Britain cannot be and should not be studied in isolation, divorced from the issues of minority mother tongues, bilingualism and English language proficiency dependent socioeconomic matters; nor can they be studied without reference to English colonialism and racism on the one hand and the contributions of the liberal and philanthropic minded volunteer and professional ESOL teachers on the other. In Helen Bishop's words:

> In looking at identity, cultural reproduction and language, the students' bilingualism needs to be seen in its political context. In some countries bilingualism is a recognised part of the culture, but in Britain and other Western countries being bilingual is a sign of being some one out of the ordinary, or a foreigner. (Bishop, 1990: 15)

The struggle for 'power and identity – ethnic and linguistic' has been part of the encounters between the minorities and the host communities in the UK. The arrival of the immigrants and refugees in the post-Second World War and post-colonial period has generated a debate, which has evolved through and with conceptual artefacts of monolingualism, multiculturalism, pluralism, bi/multilingualism, anti-racism and equal opportunities. The tension has always been between pressures to embrace English and assimilate, and desire to embrace English alongside the heritage language, and nurture, acquire, sustain and develop bilingualism and empowerment. The warning by Thorpe captures this with great precision:

> Unless practitioners are aware of the ways in which ESOL teaching can either liberate or repress, and are careful to allow the learners to be empowered through the language learning process, ESOL teaching can become racist. (Thorpe, 1994: 2)

2 Trends in Second Language Research

Introduction

In order to examine meaningfully the variation in the proficiency levels of second language learners, including the adult ESOL learners, it is essential to understand the assumptions, processes and factors of second language acquisition in both tutored and untutored settings. We should, however, always bear in mind that most of the immigrants come from multilingual backgrounds and it is in principle unfair to apply monolingual standards to measure multilingual linguistic proficiencies. The theory and practice of second language learning in the late nineteenth and greater half of the twentieth century was largely based on the behaviourist view that all human activities, including the linguistic ones, could be explained in terms of association between stimulus and response. The behaviourists' view of the human mind as a blank slate and of learning as a process of writing on it by repetition and reinforcement directed the attention of the linguists and language teachers to structure drills and contrastive analysis. It was with Chomsky's (1957, 1965, 1968) revolutionary ideas that the innateness of linguistic competence was asserted and the empty organism position came under severe criticism (Chomsky, 1959).

Traditional Approaches

As Reber (1973) points out, the associationists treat the human mind as a sort of blank blackboard on which the environment writes its message. Although there are some differences between the positions taken by Gutherie (1935), Mowrer (1954), Osgood (1963, 1968), Pavlov (1927) and Skinner (1957), the chaining of stimulus-response connections is common to all of them. The views of Jakobovits (1970), Rivers (1964), Spolsky (1966) and others on the behaviourist principles as applied to second language learning may be summarised as follows (see, for example, Hutchinson & Waters, 1987):

1. Language learning is a mechanical process of habit formation.
2. Habits are strengthened through reinforcement and reward.

3. Repetition and practice of units and their concatenation are effective ways of language performance.

4. Verbal responses are stimuli which become conditioned to and elicit other responses. These responses also have stimulus properties and the result is a chain of association links.

5. Never translate.

6. Deal new language in the sequence: hear, speak, read and write.

7. Correct all errors immediately.

The actual application of these behaviourist principles to the teaching of second languages had to wait parallel developments in structural linguistics. The method used most widely until then was the grammar-translation method. The current educational philosophy and pedagogical practice emphasised memorisation of lexical items, rules and paradigms, and translation of classical texts. The ability in the target language was measured in terms of the ability to reproduce grammatical rules and translation from the target language to the mother tongue and vice versa. Used in second/foreign language learning, this method completely ignored the spoken aspects of language; besides, it did not relate language learning to the learner's environment in any significant way. The role of the learner was largely formal and mechanical and the method left very little to the imagination of the teacher. Although translation of the above type was rejected as a language teaching strategy for a long time, it is now back into the classroom in more creative ways where the focus is not so much on accuracy but on collective translation as a strategy to utilise the resources of a multilingual classroom (see, for example, Agnihotri, 1995).

The rapid growth of structural linguistics in the early twentieth century was based on the assumption that language is a set of utterances (Bloomfield, 1926) which is learnt as a set of habits. These assumptions presumed and were supported by the behaviourist principles of learning. Structural linguistics also emphasised the supremacy of speech over writing, focused on the need of using native speakers as a part of teaching strategy and insisted that spoken language must be mastered before learning of the writing system. These psychological and linguistic considerations formed the basis of the audiolingual method of teaching second languages. As Rivers (1964) points out, memorisation and manipulation of patterns, which bring out partial resemblances beneath surface variations of vocabulary, form the psychological basis of the audiolingual approach. In this approach, grammar was not taught explicitly but was only to be inferred by the learner. The lessons were generally woven around classroom objects and day-to-day encounters. Learners were encouraged to understand the meaning of new elements through relevant contexts rather than through a bilingual vocabulary. The concomitant developments in psychology, linguistics, world trade and commerce, invention of the magnetic tape, etc. accelerated the popularity of the audiolingual method. The easy accessibility of the magnetic tape helped in popularising the audiolingual method of language learning, for with its help even a few language teachers could teach a large number of people. One of the major shortcomings of the audiolingual method was its inability to discriminate between the different types of learners. The teacher was often involved in very boring and repetitive exercises which the bright learners found meaningless and the slow learners too difficult.

Contrastive analysis

Weinreich (1953) and other linguists such as Haugen and Boas felt that individuals tend to transfer the forms, meanings and their distribution in their native language and culture to the foreign language productively and receptively. Linguists such as Fries and Lado had, however, already made similar observations about the teaching of foreign languages in the classroom:

> The most effective materials (for language teaching) are based upon a scientific description of the language to be learned carefully compared with a parallel description of the native language of the learner. (Fries, 1945: 9)

As Sridhar (1981) points out, the practical experience of foreign language teachers, studies of language contact in bilingual situations, and the associationist theories of learning converged to provide a solid foundation for the growth of contrastive analysis (see, for example, Lee, 1968; Nemser, 1971a; Nickel & Wagner, 1968). The salient feature of contrastive analysis could be summarised as:

> 1. the prime cause, or even the sole cause, of difficulty and errors in foreign language learning is interference coming from the learner's native language;
> 2. the difficulties are chiefly, or wholly, due to the differences between the two languages;
> 3. the greater these differences are, the more acute the learning difficulties would be;
> 4. the results of a comparison between the two languages are needed to predict the difficulties and errors which will occur in learning the foreign language; and
> 5. what there is to teach can best be found by comparing the two languages and then subtracting what is common to them, so that what the student has to learn equals the sum of the differences established by the contrastive analysis. (Lee, 1968: 186)

The principles and methodology of contrastive analysis came under severe criticism (Gradman, 1971; Lee, 1968; Whitman & Jackson, 1972, among others). It was suggested that contrastive analysis perpetuated an oversimplified and naive view of language learning and acquisition. It ignored the prior learning of the target language which may be as much a source of interference as the learner's first language. The predictions of errors made by contrastive analysis may not always be reliable as the learners with different linguistic backgrounds tend to make similar errors. Buteau (1970), Felix (1981), Ghadessey (1980), Oller (1972a) and Richards (1971a) have provided enough evidence to show that the source of the errors produced by the second language learners may not always be explainable in terms of interference from the native language. The continuum of same–similar–different may not be parallel to the continuum of no-problem-easy difficult. Richards (1971a) basing his analysis on a large number of empirical studies suggested that the errors could be intralingual and developmental arising out of overgeneralisation, ignorance of rule-restrictions, etc. Felix (1981: 108) has tried to show that foreign language learning under classroom conditions seems partially to follow the same set of natural processes that characterise other types of language acquisition. Though there may be an amount of truth in the claims made by Felix, it is difficult to believe that the learning situation and the learners' attitudes and motivation are irrelevant to second language learning. Most learners, whether learning a given language as a first or second language, may go through a similar structural route, but their rate of learning, learning strategies and language proficiency is likely to vary from setting to setting in relation to the relevant social and psychological variables.

Cognitive Approaches

Chomsky (1959) reacted very strongly to the associationistic principles of the behaviourists and to their uncalled for extrapolation from animal behaviour to human behaviour. He felt that behaviourism simplified the learning process and undermined the role of creativity of the human mind. It did not explain how all normal children acquired essentially comparable grammars of great complexity with a remarkable rapidity in the first language. To quote Chomsky:

> As far as acquisition of language is concerned, it seems clear that reinforcement, casual observation, and natural inquisitiveness (coupled with a strong tendency to imitate) are important factors, as is the remarkable capacity of the child to generalize, hypothesize, and 'process information' in a variety of very special, apparently highly complex ways ... which may be largely innate, or may develop through some sort of learning or through maturation of the nervous system. (Chomsky, 1959: 158)

Chomsky's ideas had very strong impact on theories of second language learning. It was asserted that the process of language learning was not additive and linear and that language was learnt as a whole act (Newmark, 1966; Newmark & Reibel, 1968). Consequently, the learner, rather than the teacher or the materials, became the focus of study; the errors made by the learner were no longer viewed as pathologies to be eradicated but were seen as necessary stages in the gradual acquisition of the target system (Richards & Sampson, 1974: 17–8). Subsequent research has viewed the learner as an active participant in the learning situation in a socio-psychological framework. Dulay & Burt (1977) presented a general overview of the process of acquisition, concentrating on the role of creativity in that process:

> No one today would deny the creative participation of the learner in the acquisition process. The combined effects of Chomsky's revival of the 'creative aspects of language use' as a major focus of theoretical linguistics, along with the complementary effects of Piaget in developmental psychology, have given creativity a central place in contemporary psycholinguistics. (Dulay & Burt, 1977: 65)

As a result of this shift from behaviourist to cognitive aspects of learning a new method of second language teaching evolved where greater emphasis was laid on acquiring conscious control of the patterns through study and analysis rather than through analogy. More and more emphasis began to be given to those exercises in teaching which would help the learner to deduce the language system and internalise the rules that govern the target language. Thus, under the influence of Gestalt psychology and transformational generative linguistics, the Cognitive Code Learning theory emerged. The psychological principles emphasised in this theory are as follows:

(1) the frequency with which an item is contrasted with other items is more important than frequency of repetition;
(2) the more meaningful the material with which the student works the greater the facility in retention;
(3) materials presented visually are more easily learned than comparable materials presented aurally; and
(4) conscious attention to critical features and understanding them will facilitate learning. (Carroll, 1966: 104-5)

> Since the difference between structuralism and the generative approach is not as profound as Chomsky and his school seems to mean – partly because they have revolted against a structuralism other than the one we had become accustomed to in Europe – the implications of this change in teaching methods is not as far reaching as some people are inclined to think. (Malmberg, 1971: 9)

However, the impact of the new cognitive approaches on the stages in the acquisition of L2 and analysis of L2 learner's output was considerable. The work of Corder (1967, 1971, 1973, 1974), Dulay & Burt (1974), Duskova (1969),

Nemser (1971a), Richards & Sampson (1974), Selinker (1969, 1972) among others showed that learners learnt a second language on its own terms and that at each stage of learning the output of the learner possessed systematic features.

Communicative Approach

Chomsky's (1965) basic concern was to characterise the native ideal speaker-hearer's competence ignoring variables that affected his performance. Hymes (1971) took Chomsky's distinction between competence and performance as a point of departure and suggested that 'communicative competence' encompassed the understanding of how to use language appropriately in given sociocultural situations. The theoretical precursors of communicative approach were Austin (1962), Halliday (1967, 1975) and Searle (1969), and it was developed by Hymes (1971), Wilkins (1972, 1974a,b, 1976) and Munby (1978). The main focus of those interested in the communicative approach was not on the repertoire of linguistic forms which the learner may need but on the communicative needs of the learner. They departed radically from the traditional grammatical syllabus by working from the 'needs' of the learner to the linguistic forms which had to be learnt if the needs were to be fulfilled. The need to identify the communicative needs of the learners led several scholars to the analysis of real life language and discourse analysis. Widdowson (1973) particularly stresses the need of going beyond the mastery of grammatical structures and developing the ability for participating in a discourse. The principles of communicative methodology have been summed up by Morrow:

(1) Know what you are doing (i.e. make sure each part of the lesson focusses on some operation the student might want to perform in the TL).

(2) The whole is more than the sum of the parts (i.e. communication cannot be broken down into its component parts without its nature being thus destroyed – what is needed is the ability to work in the context of the whole).

(3) The processes are as important as the forms (a method which aims to develop the ability of students to communicate in a foreign language will aim to replicate as far as possible the processes of communication).

(4) To learn it, do it (... the learner can learn ... only by practising to communicate).

(5) Mistakes are not always mistakes (... a communicative method must go back to first principles in deciding how it will reach its aim of developing the communicative ability of the student. It may well be that it will require the flexibility to treat different things as mistakes at different stages in the learning process). (Morrow, 1981: 100)

For Prabhu (1987) and his colleagues, the essential basis of language learning is not the acquisition of grammatical rules but an active participation in the *meaning* of different communicational tasks.

Sociolinguistic Perspective

The need for a comprehensive sociolinguistic study of the output of the second language learner becomes all the more important when questions of proficiency level, norms of correctness and instructional models are raised. As Dickerson (1974) suggests, efforts should be made to accommodate variability in the second language learner's output while testing proficiency level, and the traditional monolithic testing format should be made more flexible. The notion of error and the whole methodology of error analysis needs to be redefined. Labov (1966, 1969, 1972) made highly significant contributions towards unfolding the systematic nature of hitherto stigmatised varieties and also added new techniques of data elicitation and analysis to the repertoire of sociolinguistics and applied linguistics. As Loveday (1982) points out, the body of research which challenges the normative pedagogical tradition of second language teaching is rapidly growing, and is asserting that the so-called deviancy in L2 users' speech is contextually coherent, communicatively effective, necessarily developmental, and formally creative.

However, despite such linguistically justifiable claims for the acceptance of communicatively efficient multiple norms recognising the different varieties-dialects, sociolects, etc. instead of a monolithic standard, those involved in teaching language, especially a second language, and in the process helping the students – directly or indirectly – set up their norms, must be fully aware of the social realities and prejudices that go with such norms of language use, and strive for what eventually serves the best interest of the learner, rather than what is currently fashionable, popular or politically correct. The changing ethos of teaching/education and of its goals in Britain during the last half of this century and its implications deserve close study by those arguing for any change just because the *status quo* falls short of the ideal.

The learning situation

In addition to the linguistic and social psychological aspects, the nature of the learning situation may be very important (Gardner, 1985; Preston, 1989). Among the recent approaches claiming to theorise on the learning situations Schumann's (1978) Acculturation Model and Krashen's (1978a,b) Monitor Model are particularly important. Schumann (1978) has hypothesised that acculturation is the major causal variable in second language acquisition and that the degree to which the learner acculturates to the target language group will control the degree to which he acquires the target language. He conceives of two types of acculturation: in type one the learner is socially integrated with the TL group; in type two, the TL group acts as a reference point. In type one, the learner's original identity is not at stake. His social integration leads to sufficient contact and his psychological openness converts the input he receives into intake. It is, therefore, not enough to desire to be like the TL group; what really matters is the number and nature of opportunities a learner gets to interact in the target language. Krashen (1982) has built the acculturation model as a component of the theory of monitor model for language acquisition. The monitor hypothesis posits that acquisition and learning are used in very specific ways. Normally, acquisition results in our utterances in the second language and is the basis of our fluency. Monitor, which consists of the learning of explicit rules of grammar, comes into play as an 'editor' to correct the utterances produced by the acquired system. Though monitor has very limited use in second language learning, it has the advantage of allowing performers to supply structures and items which are not as yet acquired. It may be usefully exploited in language pedagogy in order to increase accuracy, to teach about language to interested students, and to increase confidence in the creative construction process. Krashen's comprehensive model may be represented as follows:

Input —— Affective —— LAD —— Acquired —— Output
    filter   competence

Like Schumann, Krashen also places a great emphasis on input. According to Krashen (1982), the best methods of teaching are those that supply 'comprehensible input' in 'low anxiety' situations containing messages that students really want to hear. These methods do not force early production but persuade the learners to produce only when they are ready to do so. Learning will result not from forcing and correcting production but from supplying communicative and comprehensible input. The concept of affective filter was proposed by Dulay & Burt (1977). Schumann's acculturation hypothesis is easily restatable in terms of comprehensible input and positive affective filter. Affective filter refers to factors such as motivation, self-confidence, anxiety, attitude, etc. According to Dulay & Burt:

> Among other things the socio-affective filter contributes to (a) individual preferences for certain input models over others; (b) prioritizing aspects of language to be learnt; and (c) determining when language acquisition efforts should cease. (Dulay & Burt, 1977: 68)

Recent research has brought out the inadequacy of some of Krashen's hypothesis. It is argued that no clear distinction can be made between acquisition and learning; similarly no speech is completely unmonitored. As McLaughlin (1990) points out, Krashen's Monitor Model may fail to account for individual differences in language learning as the fundamental distinction between learning and acquisition is ephemeral; these differences may arise because of language learning ability, i.e. aptitude. In fact, the kind of binary distinctions made by Krashen may not exist in reality. Input may often be partially spontaneous and partially formal; output may also often be partially monitored, even in informal settings. As Stevick (1976) points out, those whose attitudes are not optimal for second language acquisition will not only tend to seek less input but they will also have a high or strong filter – even if they understand the message they may not internalise it. Those who have more positive attitudes will have a low filter and will be more open to the input. Skehan (1989) laments the fact that a greater amount of SLA research has been concerned with the universal processes rather than individual differences. He contrasts two models of SLA, namely the Monitor Model (Krashen, 1982, 1985) and the *Good Language Learner Model* (Naiman *et al.,* 1978). The former, though more influential, has focused on shared processes in SLA, whereas the latter provides enough scope for pursuing individual differences research.

Recent work in the Universal Grammar (such as Chomsky, 1988) has made a distinction between principles and parameters of language learning. Principles refer to those aspects of human language which are available to all human beings, whereas parameters are posited to account for differences obtaining in human languages. Cook (1991) summarises the implications of this distinction for second language teaching. We do not need to teach principles such as structure dependency because they are universal. On the other hand, we should create optimal exposure for triggering parameters and for building structural frames for different lexical items.

The Learner

The humanistic and psychological shift of focus from the teacher and teaching material to the learner has led the research investigators to identify those learner variables which appear to be responsible for success or failure in second language learning. Significant among the learner variables identified are: age, intelligence, aptitude, cognitive style, personality, attitudes, and motivation.

Age

Penfield (1953) suggested that the human brain loses its plasticity after puberty. He argued that children relearn their language after injury or disease. Burstall (1975) mentions that there is no experimental evidence available to support the neuro-physiological position taken by Penfield (1953) and Lenneberg

(1967). Ramsey & Wright (1974) showed that children who arrived in Canada under the age of seven fared better at learning English than those who arrived late. Several other studies of immigrants such as Agnihotri (1979) showed similar results. It has been suggested that lateralisation makes the brain-function to become specialised in the early teens. Another explanation given for the Penfieldian position is cognitive development. Cook (1978) quotes the work of Tremaine (1975) who correlates the transition to the early Piagetian stage of 'concrete operations' at about seven with the syntactic development of bilingual children. Seliger (1978) points out that there is much evidence to show that children acquire the phonological systems of another language much better than adults, and proposes the concept of multiple critical periods correlating with localisation and the gradual loss of plasticity.

It appears that language acquisition abilities are not lost at once. There is only a gradual reduction of such abilities. Several studies, such as Asher & Price (1967), Olson & Samuels (1973) have shown that adults are actually better learners than children. To quote Cook:

> Far from showing superiority of children, most of the hard evidence warrants the opposite conclusion: adults are better than children at learning a second language when tests are conducted under controlled conditions. (Cook, 1978: 30)

The fact that child immigrants often learn the language of the host society better than adult immigrants may be attributed not only to the adult's loss of plasticity of mind but also to the differences in situations, attitudes, motivation and pressure from peer group. Macnamara (1973) makes a distinction between formal and structured classroom learning and learning in the street. The motivation of an immigrant child to be recognised as a member of the group he wishes to belong to is generally far stronger than the adult whose primary motivations may largely be instrumental. Agnihotri's (1979) study showed that native speakers failed to distinguish the migrant Sikh children from the British children on the basis of their recorded speech.

Intelligence

Jakobovits (1970) points out that intelligence is usually conceived of as the ability to learn and consists of verbal ability, reasoning ability, concept formation ability, etc. Intelligence tests generally consist of abstract and quasi-mathematical problems and it is often difficult to say whether they measure recent learning, genetic transmission of knowledge or early infant experience. Such tests may be useful as a measure of mental age of a population, but it is doubtful if their scores can be used to predict the ability to acquire languages. According to

Jakobovits (1970), intelligence contributes to 15 to 20% variance in performance. Pimsleur *et al.* (1962) report on a large number of studies examining the correlation of intelligence and verbal ability with foreign language learning. Though the correlations were generally positive, many studies seem sceptical. Carroll points out:

> Within very broad limits, IQ or 'intelligence' is a correlate of foreign language success, but it is much less related to foreign language success than it is to many other types of school courses. Generally, foreign language teachers have been disappointed in the attempt to use intelligence test scores as predictors of foreign language success. One possible reason for the low validity of intelligence measures in this application is the fact that intelligence is actually very complex. Most of the commonly employed intelligence tests measure a number of abilities simultaneously – verbal ability, reasoning ability, memory ability, and others. While a few of these abilities may be relevant to foreign language success, most are not and their net effect is to depress the correlation of intelligence with foreign language success. (Carroll & Sapon, 1959: 22)

Aptitude

Aptitude has been defined as the disposition to be able to do something. The note of caution which was raised in the case of intelligence is valid for aptitude tests also. Do they measure early experience or inherent abilities? The three best known measures of FL aptitude tests for native speakers of English are the Modern Language Aptitude Test (MLAT) developed by Carroll & Sapon (1959), The Pimsleur Language Aptitude Battery (LAB) (1966), and the York Language Aptitude test developed by Green (1977). MLAT consists of: (1) phonetic coding ability to code and store sounds; (2) grammatical sensitivity; (3) rote memory for foreign materials; and (4) the ability to infer linguistic patterns from new materials. Gardner & Lambert (1965) found that different dimensions of foreign language skills are related to different components of aptitude. It was noticed that verbal reasoning was related to foreign language achievement especially when it measured students' ability to recognise linguistic materials. Phonetic coding ability helped one to learn vocabulary, and the knowledge of grammatical distinctions in one's native language will help the students to do well in a foreign language. Jakobovits (1970) suggests that subcomponents of FL aptitude may be exploited usefully in foreign language teaching since, though they correlate significantly with achievement, the internal correlation of the components is not significantly high. Thus, an individual may be high on phonetic coding ability but low on grammatical sensitivity or rote-memorisation. The teacher who has the information about the aptitude configuration of his student can modify his instructional materials accordingly.

Cognitive style

Though its conclusive and extensive investigation is still awaited, the cognitive style with which the learner organises his universe may be an important determiner of the language learning process. The information processing habits of the learner will provide insights into the interaction between the learner's cognitive style and the subject matter. As Brown (1973: 238) points out, cognitive style refers to 'self-consistent and enduring individual differences in cognitive organisation and functioning'. Four specific variables identified within the cognitive style are: (a) reflective–impulsive thinking; (b) broad–narrow categorising; (c) skeletonising–embroidering; and (d) belief congruence–contradiction. Brown quotes some studies (such as Kagan, 1965) to show that reflective students are slower and more accurate readers than conceptually impulsive students.

Personality

As Nida (1958) points out, too much attention has been paid to such outside factors as the teacher, teaching method and material. He suggests that a better understanding of the causes of learning a foreign language can be found by examining some of the more subtle and less obvious conditions relating to the personality of the learner. Personality traits such as extroversion and introversion, assertiveness, emotional stability, social conformity, anxiety, placidity, etc. have generally been ignored in second language research. (For a complete list of the 16 primary personality factors, see *Manual for the 16PF*, Champaign, IL: The Institute for Personality and Ability Testing, 1972.) Several studies such as Bartz (1974), Pimsleur *et al.* (1964), Smart *et al.* (1970), Wittenborn & Larson (1944) and Wittenborn *et al.* (1945) have attempted to investigate the relationship between personality traits and language learning. Pimsleur *et al.* (1964) compared average achievers and under-achievers in high schools. Social conformity, extroversion, flexibility and tolerance for ambiguity were some of the characteristics that a successful foreign language student was assumed to have. The study did not yield any significantly positive result. Bartz (1974: 125) showed that introversion, soberness and self-sufficiency correlated significantly with oral components of communicative competence and students with 'traits of imagination, placidness and low anxiety tended to score higher on the written components of the communicative competence tests'. The instruments generally used to investigate the relationship between personality traits and foreign language learning have generally not been very systematic and their construction has been guided by intuition rather than by any theory or empirical investigation. To quote Leino:

Little information is available on the reliability and validity of the instruments and the generalizability of the results is further limited by the small number of subjects especially in the studies where high and low achievers have been compared. The subjects in the majority of studies have been university students; so there may have been selection even as to personality traits. (Leino, 1972: 9)

The question whether certain personality traits help language learning is still open. Does a child who causes nuisance in the class because of his adventurous nature prove to be a better language learner? Does the ability to entertain conflicting ideas correlate significantly with language learning ability?

Attitudes

A considerable amount of research has been done on the relationship between such psychological variables as attitudes and motivation, and proficiency in learning a second language. In general, positive attitude towards a second language and its speakers appears to be associated with high proficiency in second language. Burstall (1975) quotes several studies which show a positive correlation between attitudes and achievement. But she is sceptical of the causal relationships between the two. She quotes the NFER evaluation which shows that an early achievement in French affected later attitudes towards and achievement in French to a significantly greater extent than early attitudes towards French affected the subsequent development of either attitude or achievement. The initial success or failure in language learning may, thus, be a powerful determinant of linguistic attitudes and achievements.

Two basic concepts introduced in this connection are those of authoritarianism and ethnocentrism. Authoritarianism refers to anti-democratic feelings and is generally measured through respect for authority, use of force, nationalism, etc. (see Forms 45 and 40 of the California F-Scale, Adorno *et al.,* 1950). Ethnocentrism, on the other hand, refers to people who are suspicious of or prejudiced towards foreign people and ideas, and is generally measured through attitudes towards the foreigners, preservation of nationality, respect for national symbols, etc. (see E-Scale , Adorno *et al.,* 1950). To quote Gardner & Lambert:

Learners who have strong ethnocentric or authoritarian attitude or who have learned to be prejudiced toward foreign peoples are unlikely to approach the language learning task with an integrative outlook. (Gardner & Lambert, 1972: 16)

Lambert and his associates at McGill University conducted a series of studies (Anisfeld & Lambert, 1961; Feenstra & Gardner, 1968; Gardner & Lambert, 1959; Lambert *et al.,* 1962; Peal & Lambert, 1962) to investigate the effects of 'psychological preparedness' involving attitudinal and motivational factors, on second language learning (see Gardner & Lambert, 1972).

In their three American studies (Louisiana, Maine and Connecticut) Gardner & Lambert established that

a friendly outlook towards the other group whose language is being learned can differentially sensitise the learner to the audio-lingual features of the language, making him more perceptive to forms of pronunciation and accent than is the case for a learner without this open and friendly disposition. If the students' attitude is highly ethnocentric and hostile, we have seen that no progress to speak of will be made in acquiring any aspect of the language. Such a student not only is perceptually insensitive to the language, but apparently is also unwilling to modify or adjust his own response system to approximate the new pronunciational responses required in the other language. (Gardner & Lambert, 1972: 134)

Their French-American studies also showed that positive attitudes towards French-American culture coupled with favourable stereotypes of the European French were associated with certain expressive skills in French (see Gardner & Lambert, 1972: chap. 5). Using the now well-known 'matched guise technique' they showed that the American adolescents studying French had pejorative and biased images of typical representatives of the ethnolinguistic groups whose language they were supposed to master. Lambert & Gardner pointed out the pedagogical implications of such stereotypes:

One can imagine the difficulties a French teacher would have in her attempts to penetrate and modify these images. The need to systematically modify these images, distorted as they certainly are, becomes very evident, since negative stereotypes of this sort, if accepted by a majority of students, could sabotage any educational effort to teach the language of the group in question. (Gardner & Lambert, 1972: 140)

For Giles and his associates (Scherer & Giles, 1979), the perceived distance from the target language group and stereotypes about it are as important as the real distance between the ingroup and outgroup. Higher levels of proficiency are associated with weak ingroup identification, balanced intergroup comparison, open perception of ingroup boundaries and strong identification with other social groups.

Motivation

In the social psychological approach outlined here, the learner's motivation to learn a foreign language will depend on his attitudes and his willingness to identify with the linguistic and non-linguistic features that characterise the personal advantages. Gardner & Lambert (1959) and Lambert et al. (1962) point out that foreign language learning is likely to be lower if the underlying motivation is instrumental rather than integrative. Burstall (1975) examined the hypothesis in the course of NFER evaluation of the teaching of French in primary schools and found only partial support for the view put forward by Gardner & Lambert. Although pupils' attitude and achievement proved to be closely associated, motivational characteristics of individual pupils appeared to be neither exclusively integrative nor instrumental. The majority of the pupils in the experiment shared integrative motivation evincing a strong desire for contact with French people, while at the same time giving ample evidence of instrumental motivation in the emphasis placed on the 'pay off' value of learning French in terms of enhanced employment opportunities. It is interesting to note that in the Philippines study reported in Gardner & Lambert (1972) the authors considerably distanced themselves from their original position. It appeared that in settings where there was an urgency about mastering a second language for utilitarian ends, the instrumental approach dominated the learning process. As Leino (1974) points out, the socio-psychological theory of foreign language learning started from Mowrer's (1954) concept of identification, which referred to the tendency of the child to imitate the parents in first language development. In foreign/second language learning this process is extended to the target language group. The integratively motivated student learns the foreign language because he finds the language pleasant and interesting and because he strongly wishes to enter into an active interaction with the target language speakers. Gardner & Lambert (1972) contrasted this integrative motivation with instrumental motivation which is characterised by utilitarian objectives such as obtaining admission to a particular course or getting a better job. To quote:

> This cross-cultural support for the importance of motivational and attitudinal dispositions strengthens our confidence in the basic notions we started with. But still the Philippines investigation changed our perspective on the instrumental–integrative contrast. We see now that the typical student of foreign languages in North America will profit more if he is helped to develop an integrative outlook towards the group whose language is being offered. For him, an instrumental approach has little significance and little motive force. However, for members of ethnic minority groups in North America as for those living in nations that have imported prestigious world languages and made them important national languages, the picture changes. Learning a second language of national or world wide significance is then indispensable and both instrumental and integrative orientations towards the learning task must be developed. (Gardner & Lambert, 1972: 141–2)

Exposure

One of the important components of the learner's situation is the language he hears around him. Hatch (1976) and Larsen-Freeman (1976) have shown the significance of the links between the learner's language and the types of inter-action he takes part in. Several studies conducted in India (Agnihotri *et al.*, 1988; Khanna, 1983; Khanna & Agnihotri, 1982; Mathur, 1991; Sahgal, 1983; Sawhney, 1997, among others) have shown the overwhelming importance of such social variables as exposure, schooling, parental encouragement, patterns of language use, etc. in second language learning.

Socioeconomic status

As Loveday (1982) points out, the effect of social class membership on the development of second language skills has not been fully explored. There are, however, indications that positive attitudes towards learning a second language is associated with high socioeconomic status (Burstall *et al.*, 1974). Burstall (1975) quotes several studies, such as Douglas (1964) and Robinson (1971), to show that children with parents in high status occupation tend to receive more parental support when they approach a new learning experience than do those with parents in lower status occupation.

Sex

Several studies of first language acquisition (Douglas, 1964; Morris, 1966 and others) have shown girls to be better learners than boys. Trudgill (1974) showed that women used the prestige variants more frequently than men, and related this phenomenon to female social insecurity. In a study of Panjabi migrant children in England, Agnihotri (1979) showed that girls assimilated the prestige variants faster than the boys; they were also better at resisting the stigmatised variants. Satyanath (1982) too found that Kannadiga women in Delhi showed a higher percentage of assimilation of linguistic features associated with Hindi and also a higher degree of usage than men. He found that younger women assimilated the host society's language and culture maximally. Unlike Trudgill (1974) and Mukherjee (1980) who hold social insecurity to be responsible for greater use of prestige variants, Satyanath attributes it to the sociocultural aspects of the Kannadiga community which provides women a greater opportunity of inter-action with the host society. However, in the field of formal foreign language learning there are only a few studies investigating sex as a variable. Carroll (1963), Nisbet & Welsh (1972) and Burstall *et al.* (1974) generally found girls to be better learners. Burstall (1975) points to an interesting possible relation-ship between sex differences and socioeconomic status. This NFERA (National Foundation for Educational Research) study revealed that the most marked sex differences were found in those secondary schools whose intake was predomi-nantly drawn from the lower socioeconomic strata.

Time spent

Carroll (1963a) has suggested that the total amount of time spent on a given language is an important variable in the learning process. According to Titone (1977), while children will benefit from a more extended period of time in order to be able to digest new behavioural materials like language skills, adults will be able to profit from intensive courses due to their high degree of transfer ability. Concluding her discussion of factors affecting foreign language learning, Burstall writes:

> Thus, the most conservative interpretation which the available evidence would appear to permit is that achievement of skills in a foreign language is primarily a function of the amount of time spent studying that language ... (Burstall, 1975: 21)

Second language acquisition studies of adult immigrants

Most of the studies reported in this section are from Perdue (1984: 43–67). In France, broadly speaking, two traditions are represented in existing studies on spontaneous second language acquisition by adults: the contrastive analysis and interlanguage studies. Morsly (1976), Pichel (1980) and Santos-Pereira (1981) studied the spoken French of Arabic-, Spanish- and Portuguese-speaking adult immigrants (for these studies, see Perdue, 1984). These studies are based on a contrastive analysis of the linguistic systems of the relevant language pairs in order to ascertain the relative weightage of the SL system and of the linguistic system of the TL system. Morsly & Vasseur (1976) looked at the learner's variety as a system in its own right and attempted to show from data obtained from Arabic- and Portuguese-speaking workers that the explanatory power of the contrastive-interference approach may be less than had been supposed. They suggested that the persistent linguistic problems evidenced by these informants should be related to psychological, social and economic aspects of their lives as immigrant workers. In Germany, systematic research on SLA of migrant workers began with Clyne (1968). Subsequently two projects dealing with untutored acquisition of adult migrant workers were undertaken. The aim of the first project was to describe and explain the untutored acquisition of German by Italian, Spanish and Portuguese adults in a natural setting and to determine the influence of social environment, attitudes and motivation in order to answer the question: 'Which elements constitute an "interlanguage" and which factors determine an "interlanguage"?' (Clahsen, 1980: 55). The second project dealt with the untutored SLA of adult Spanish workers. The primary aim was to describe the linguistic structure and development of learner varieties and to analyse how the learner's social and psychological background influences the acquisition process and contributes to a better foundation of language teaching.

Most of the research in spontaneous second language acquisition in Holland has dealt with the use of Dutch by foreigners, and most of these studies have dealt with syntax, with great attention being paid to word order. As reported in Perdue (1984), Jansen & Lalleman (1980a,b), and Jansen *et al.* (1981) treat the placement of pre- and post-positions and the placement of the verbs in the Dutch of Turkish and Moroccan male adults. The main question in their research was to what degree features of word order were influenced by structural features of the respective source languages. Hulstijn (1982) researched on how adult learners of Dutch handled subject/verb inversion in declarative main clauses and final placement of the verb in subordinate clauses. His research focused, however, on the question of how speech monitoring is influenced by the factors such as time pressure, attention, degree of explicit knowledge of rules and degree of impulsivity. A group of researchers identified as WTBW (1980) carried out a research on the language attitudes and language proficiency of 20 Moroccan male adults who had spent 2 to 11 years in The Netherlands. The main findings of the research revealed that there was a connection between language attitudes and language proficiency levels. It also revealed that the Moroccans appeared to speak better Dutch the younger they were, the shorter their length of stay in The Netherlands, the more school work they did, the less formal L2 training they had had, and the more Dutch friends they had.

Some studies have also shown that even when adult immigrants acquire the target grammatical structure, they sometimes impose their sociocultural meanings on them. These differences, combined with the native speaker's indifference, may often result in what Singh *et al.* (1988) call 'communicational asynchronies'. Weigel & Weigel (1985) showed how a black migrant agricultural community in the United States deviated from the standard middle-class use of directives, i.e. imperatives, imbedded imperatives and needs statements. Similarly Jaworski's (1994) study showed how Polish learners of English imposed native sociocultural patterns in responding to such formulaic greetings as 'How are you?'.

The Department of Linguistics, University of Stockholm researched on aspects of language structure and language use in learning Swedish as a second language by adult immigrants in Sweden. Aspects of lexical structure, morphology and basic syntax were studied in a functional perspective combining error analysis with typological studies. This project established a typological profile of Swedish and related it to the major immigrant languages in Sweden. Hyltenstam (1977) deals with the acquisition of Swedish negation by adult second language learners. Kotsinas (1980), reported in Perdue (1984), discusses varieties of Swedish spoken by adult Greek immigrants who had acquired Swedish outside the classroom. Several studies of adult immigrant second language acquisition have supported the L1-path hypothesis as proposed, among others, by Dulay & Burt (1974), Felix (1981) and Flynn & Espinal (1985). For example, Sadighi

(1994) showed that the acquisition of English restrictive relative clauses by Chinese, Japanese and Korean immigrants in the US followed a uniform pattern predicted by universal grammar properties; it is important to remember that relativisation in English is post-nominal, whereas in Chinese, Japanese and Korean, it is pre-nominal.

There has been considerable research effort into the acquisition of English as a second language in Britain, the US and other English-speaking countries, although most of this research has been directed at second language acquisition within tutored contexts. There has, however, been very little study of the acquisition of English by adult immigrants in spontaneous settings. In the US, as Grosjean (1982) has so effectively shown, the general attitude of the Anglo-American majority has been that members of linguistic minorities should integrate themselves into the English-speaking society as quickly as possible. According to him, the ESL courses were organised for the immigrants, but the type of English taught was academic and did not relate to their everyday lives. One of the earliest studies of the acquisition of English by senior school Panjabi children was done in 1974 (see Agnihotri, 1979). This study showed that age at arrival and length of stay were some of the most important determinants of acquiring the local Yorkshire speech. It also showed that patterns of host culture and language were not acquired at the cost of native identity. In fact, a Panjabi Sikh child assimilates British language and culture without ceasing to be a Sikh. Even as more Yorkshire English is learnt, adolescents develop a mixed Panjabi-English code for intragroup communication. There are a few British empirical studies of language use by adult immigrants. The empirical research into interaction between English native speakers and South Asian English speakers was undertaken by the National Centre for Industrial Language Training (NCILT) in collaboration with Gumperz and is described in Gumperz et al. (1980), Gumperz & Roberts (1978) and Gumperz et al. (1979). These studies coordinated by NCILT (Gumperz et al., 1980) made an extensive need analysis of the second language speakers and also examined their preferred learning strategies. The Linguistic Minority Project (LMP, Institute of Education, University of London) examined the changing patterns of bilingualism in several regions in England. This research looked into the data of Panjabi and Italian adults who had not received any regular language tuition: it is reported in Saifulla Khan (1980). Research has also been conducted into the needs and expectations of Asian redundant workers (Furnborough et al., 1982). The project on doctor–patient communication skills examined the discourse of second language speaking doctors which was used for preparing pedagogic materials (Candlin et al., 1974).

What can we learn from these diverse studies of adult immigrants learning the language of the host society? So far as the acquisition of the grammar of a second language is concerned, it seems clear that the teachers and language professionals need not worry too much about the interference phenomenon. The innate potential of universal grammar among adults does not degenerate with age; if anything it may get further accentuated because of its enormous cognitive enrichment. L2 acquisition by adult immigrants will take the route that it must. The studies of the pragmatic and social psychological aspects unfold a different story. Adult immigrants may often impose their own sociocultural meanings on the L2 grammatical structures they acquire, and it is here that the native speakers' level of empathy has an important role to play. The burden of communication is not entirely an immigrant's responsibility (he or she is already disadvantaged in a variety of ways). What is needed is not pity, sympathy or tolerance but understanding, respect and equality.

Purpose of the Present Study

Second or foreign language learning is, thus, an extremely complex process involving among other things the contributions made by the learner and the learner's environment. It would be naive to suggest that any one social or psychological variable can be the sole determinant of achievement in second language learning. The present study has been designed to investigate the relationship between some social psychological dimensions of the adult ESOL learners in the UK and their achievement in English as assessed by their teachers.

3 Method: Sample, Tools and Procedure

Introduction

The primary purpose of this pilot study was to examine the role of individual and social variables in learning English as a second language by a sample of ESOL learners at Adult Education Centres in Britain. We hoped that our analysis would have significant pedagogical implications and give us insight into the relationship between SLA theory and practice. We also decided to conduct in-depth interviews of ESOL practitioners and administrators in order to have a comprehensive picture of the issues relating to ESOL in Britain.

Exploratory Visits

The present study was started in April 1989. Before finalising our tools for data elicitation we decided to visit some ESOL centres in order to understand the socio-cultural background of the learners, their levels of proficiency in English and the teaching strategies and evaluation procedures used by the ESOL teachers. Our discussions with the ESOL teachers and the students made the following things clear:

- ESOL learners belonged to diverse ethnic and sociolinguistic backgrounds, having different mother tongues and highly variable levels of proficiency in English.
- Most of the ESOL learners were adults above the age of 25 years and the majority of them were females.
- Women generally outnumbered men at these ESOL centres. The centres could be seen as agents of social change where immigrant women, who were generally confined to household activities, found opportunities to interact with members outside their family and community.
- The teaching–learning situation was significantly informal as compared to the formal learning situation of a school classroom. Very often the learners brought their children along to the centres.
- The size of the ESOL classes was usually small (10–15 students) even though the enrolment number was generally much higher. These neigh-

bourhood centres which had an informal atmosphere did not insist on regular attendance.

- Teaching strategies used in the classes could broadly be characterised as communicative.
- The centres did not have any fixed curriculum. Each centre evolved its own curriculum based on the tutors' understanding and perception of the needs of the learners.
- In addition, in terms of material production, each centre produced its own materials and/or adapted the available ESL/EFL materials.
- No formal examination was conducted to evaluate the progress of the learners. Teachers monitored the progress of the students by keeping a record of learners' performance on different learning tasks. Frequent discussions with the learners about their work helped to integrate evaluation into teaching.
- Few ESOL centres used any widely recognised system of accreditation to record the level of proficiency achieved by the learners.

Procedure

A list of ESOL centres was prepared and letters were written to the heads of these centres stating the objectives of the proposed survey and seeking their permission to carry out the survey at their centres. A favourable response was received from most of the ESOL centres.

A questionnaire was first prepared in English and then translated into Urdu, Hindi, Bengali and Chinese. Because the learners came from different linguistic backgrounds with varied levels of proficiency in English, we tried, as far as possible, to administer the questionnaires in the mother tongues of the learners. The translations were done by proficient bilinguals. All the mother tongue questionnaires included the English version as well. The questionnaires were often completed with the help of either the tutor or the investigator. In some cases we also engaged bilingual interpreters who, in addition to English and one of the mother tongues of the learners, could handle language varieties related to the learners' mother tongues. These bilingual interpreters were very helpful both in explaining and filling in the questionnaires.

Sample

Although the questionnaires were administered to over 200 ESOL learners, the final sample consisted of 133 ESOL learners (90 females, 43 males) drawn from 13 Adult and Community Education ESOL centres located in Edinburgh, York, Leeds, Bradford, Walsall, London and Cardiff. The remaining informants either did not respond to or left the questionnaires incomplete. Over 77% of these informants were in the age group 15–46, the total age range being 15–68. Most of them (99 out of 133) had been in England for less than 10 years. Only 7 out of the 133 informants were illiterate. Others had educational qualifications equivalent to or higher than 'O' level. Most of them came from families with poor educational background and with limited use of English. (For details of sample and its social psychological profile, see Chapter 4.) The sample did not include ESOL learners in FE colleges or those who were following workplace based vocational courses often funded by Manpower Services Commission.

Materials

The tools consisted of a Questionnaire (Appendix I) divided into four subsections. Questions 1–14 were designed to elicit the sociolinguistic background of the informants; questions 15–25 sought to elicit the learners' patterns of language use in different domains of activity; questions 26–33 were aimed at discovering linguistic attitudes and motivational orientation and intensity of the learners; and questions 34–36 were meant to elicit the learners' social stereotypes of his own, of the host and of an ideal community. We also designed a rating sheet for the evaluation of English skills of the learners by the tutors (Appendix II); and a semi-structured questionnaire (Appendix III) was prepared for an in-depth interview of the tutors/administrators.

Scoring Procedure

On the basis of the data elicited through these questions the following sociolinguistic and proficiency variables were isolated and quantified on appropriate scales.

Individual and social variables

Age
The actual age was treated as a continuous variable. Age is a function of 'age at arrival' and 'length of stay'.

Age at arrival: Continuous variable.

Length of stay in the UK: Continuous variable.

Sex: male = 1; female = 2.

Occupation: It ranged from 'unemployed' to 'professional'.

Occupation	Scale
Unemployed	0
Student/Housewife	1
Unskilled labour	2
Skilled labour/small business	3
Professionals	4

Education of the family: The following scale was used to quantify the detailed information about the level of education of different members of the family.

Level of education	Scale
Uneducated	0
Semi-educated	1
Educated	2
Highly educated	3

Each family was located on this scale and an average percentage score was obtained for each country.

Education of the informant: The informants ranged from being illiterate to holders of degrees. The following scale was used to quantify their educational qualifications.

Level of education	Scale
Illiterate	0
Primary	1
Middle	2
Matric ['O' level]	3
Senior Sec. ['A' level]	4
BA/equivalent degree	5
MA and above	6

Rating of parents' English skills: Informants were asked to use a 4-point scale (ranging from 0–3) to rate separately each of their parent's ability to use each of the four skills of English. Thus, each parent could get a maximum score of 12 and minimum of 0. However, the scores of both the parents were combined and introduced as one composite variable.

Self-rating of mother tongue skills: Each informant was asked to rate his ability to use the four skills of his mother tongue on a 4-point scale. These scores could thus range from 0–12.

Self-rating of English skills: The method used for rating parents' English skills was also used to rate one's own proficiency in English in the four skills.

Patterns of the language use: Informants were asked to indicate all the languages spoken at home and indicate how often they used each one of them in terms of the following scale:

Frequency	Scale
Never	0
Sometimes	1
Every day	2

Patterns of language use in the family: The informants were asked to *indicate* the language(s) they used with their husbands/wives, parents, grandparents, brothers, sisters, children below the age of five and children above the age of five. Their responses were elicited on a scale ranging from using a 'considerable' amount of English, to 'little' and 'none' at all. The following scale was used:

Amount of English used	Scale
None	0
A little	1
Considerable	2

The informants provided this information in respect of seven different relations living together; thus the maximum score could be 14 and the minimum 0. This also helped us to estimate the use of mother tongue in different domains.

Patterns of language use outside the family: Unlike in the previous question, the informants were asked to indicate the languages they used when talking to relatives not living with them, talking to friends and neighbours, writing personal letters to friends and relatives, talking to doctors, and to people at religious places and shops.

Confidence in the use of English: The informants were asked to indicate whether they had any difficulty in speaking in English to their child's teacher, government officials, shop assistants, employees of public transport or other services; in understanding TV programmes, in talking to doctors, reading the instructions on the medicine labels, official letters, documents, newspapers and magazines. If they stated that they had no difficulty they were given a score of 1 each, and if they had difficulty they were given 0.

Watching programmes in English on TV: Informants were asked to indicate how often they watched various programmes in English. The following scale was used to quantify the answers:

Frequency	Scale
Never	0
Sometimes	1
Often	2

Listening to programmes in English on radio: The informants were asked to indicate how often they listened to various programmes in English. A scale similar to the one used for watching programmes on the TV was used.

English used at work: Informants were also asked to indicate the languages they used with their workmates, employers and members of public while they were at work. The responses were quantified as below:

Amount of English used	Scale
None	0
Some	1
Considerable	2

As the responses were elicited separately for each category of people at work, the maximum score could be 6 and the minimum 0.

Importance of improving English language skills: Informants were asked to indicate how important it was for them to improve their competence in the use of the four skills of English. The relative importance of each skill was quantified as below:

Level of importance	Scale
Not at all important	0
Important	1
Very important	2

The maximum score for the four skills could be 8.

Desire to improve the mother tongue skills: The informants were asked to indicate whether or not they would like to improve their ability to use their heritage language. If they wished to improve their competence in their heritage language skills they were given a score of 1, otherwise a score of 0.

Attitude and motivation

Attitude towards English language: Following Gardner & Lambert (1972), a number of questions eliciting attitudes and motivation of the ESOL learners were included in the questionnaire. In order to find out the informants' attitude towards English language, five popular linguistic attributes generally used in relation to the English language, namely, 'sweet', 'scientific', 'civilized', 'useful' and 'easy' were used. Out of these five, three attributes were positively worded and two negatively. Each of these attributes was evaluated on a 3-point scale, ranging from 'very much' to 'not at all'. Scoring for the positive and negative attributes was done as below:

	Positive	Negative
Very much	3	1
A little	2	2
Not at all	1	3

The scores could vary between 0 and 15.

Desire to learn English: The informants were asked to indicate how much English they would like to be used in their English class, how often they would use English outside school, and how interesting they find learning English. Responses through multiple choice items were used to elicit these answers and were evaluated on a 3-point scale ranging from 1 to 3. Thus, the maximum score could be 9 and minimum 3.

Motivational intensity: The informants were asked to indicate how often they liked to answer questions in an English class, how much enthusiasm they had for doing extra English assignments, and how often they sought the help of the teacher in their English classes. As in the case of attitudes towards English language, the responses were elicited through multiple choice items and evaluated on a 3-point scale. Thus, the maximum score for the motivational intensity could be 9 and the minimum 3.

Integrative orientation: The following reasons were identified as indicative of integrative orientation:

(1)   To understand better the English-speaking people and their way of life.
(2)   To gain friends more easily among the English-speaking people.
(3)   To meet and interact with the English-speaking people.
(4)   To think and behave as the English do.
(5)   To study English literature.

The learners were asked to indicate how important these reasons were for them for learning English. Each item was measured on a 3-point scale ranging between 0–2. A high score for such orientation (maximum = 10) would reflect the informant's acceptance of the integrative reasons for studying English.

Instrumental orientation: This orientation stressed the pragmatic or utilitarian reasons for learning English and was elicited through the following five reasons for learning language:

(1)   To become independent.
(2)   To go into business.
(3)   To get a good job.
(4)   To get quick promotion in the profession.
(5)   To acquire educational qualification.

A high score of such orientation (maximum = 10) would imply informants subscribing to the instrumental value of learning English.

Social stereotypes: Stereotypes of the British people, their language community, and the ideal community which they would like to be members of were elicited through a 16-item scale used separately for each group. Nine items were positively worded and seven negatively. Each attribute on the scale was scored on a 0–2 scale. Thus, a high score (maximum = 32) for each community would indicate a positive attitude towards it. Three different scores indicating each individual's stereotypes of the three groups were introduced as separate variables.The ESOL classes had learners of various levels of proficiency, ranging from being able to greet someone to carry out a small transaction in a department store or errand in a place of work. Instead of having a formal evaluation of their learners' proficiency in English, it was felt that the tutors' evaluation should be considered a reliable measure of proficiency. Thus, every tutor was taken into confidence and asked to evaluate each of their students on all the four skills of listening, speaking, reading and writing English on a 4-point scale (0–3) ranging from 'not at all' to 'very well'. Thus, a learner could get a maximum score of 12 and minimum of 0. The instructors were also asked to give any additional information, which they felt was relevant and necessary to reveal the ESOL skills the learners had and their style or speed of learning.

Teachers' profile

In order to have a comprehensive view of ESOL in Britain it was considered equally important to have tutors'/administrators' views on issues affecting teaching and learning of ESOL. Thus, most tutors/administrators at the ESOL centres, selected for the survey discussed earlier, were interviewed extensively, and the interviews were recorded with the permission of the interviewee. In addition to finding information about the background of the ESOL centres, the interviewees were asked questions about their educational qualifications, whether they were temporary or permanent employees, how long they had been teaching ESOL classes, etc. After this preliminary information each tutor/administrator was asked to give his/her views on the following issues.

- Strategies/methods of teaching ESOL: Use of the monolingual or bilingual method
- Needs analysis of the ESOL learners
- Curriculum/syllabus and teaching materials, adaptation of EFL/ESOL material
- Evaluation and assessment: RSA profile accreditation or some other award
- Teachers' evaluation
- Recruitment and training of ESOL teachers
- Status of ESOL at present, and the future of ESOL in Britain and Europe
- Regional variation of ESOL and networking
- Distinctions between ESL, ESOL and EFL
- Difficulties experienced by the ESOL teachers
- Social perception about ESOL
- Funding of ESOL teaching
- Resources for ESOL teaching

4 Social and Psychological Aspects of ESOL Learners

Introduction

In this chapter we first briefly provide a description of ESOL centres and then give a fairly detailed socio-psychological profile of ESOL learners in terms of their country of origin, age and gender distribution, occupational patterns, age at arrival and length of stay in the UK, educational background, claimed control of English and the mother tongue, teachers' evaluation, exposure through mass-media, patterns of language use, social and linguistic stereotypes, motivational orientation and motivational intensity.

ESOL Centres

At least in theory, ESOL centres are not supposed to be mere English language teaching institutions. They function as support centres which try to understand and appreciate the needs and aspirations of the multiethnic, multilingual and multicultural learners, and prepare them not only for better employment oppor-tunities but also equip them with access skills for social, leisure and recreational purposes. ESOL centres also offer feeder courses for subsequent advanced classes which learners may like to attend. The centres very consciously aim to have an overall anti-racist perspective. The tutors find most of the existing EFL curri-culum, syllabi and materials unsuitable for ESOL learners as well as often incompatible with their stated goal. They feel that a suitable curriculum can be evolved only through careful negotiation with the learners.

Most of these centres are located in neighbourhood areas dominated by immigrant populations. The majority of the students are female and between 16 and 45 years of age. The centres are generally located in church halls, schools, clinics or community centres which often are run-down buildings. The classes are generally held twice a week and each class is of at least two hours duration. However, some intensive classes are conducted for 10 hours a week for a period of 10 weeks. Most centres provide creche facilities for the learners' children (under-fives). The teaching hours are generally flexible and timetabled to be convenient for the learners. When the new learners arrive, their existing levels of proficiency in English are assessed before they are admitted to the course.

A majority of the teachers at these centres are part-time/voluntary white teachers. These teachers undergo a brief period of training which amounts to 10 hours spread over a period of five to six weeks. There is great variation in the contents of and approaches to training. On the whole, the training focuses on sensitivity to other cultures and languages, problems of adjustment to the new community, equal opportunities for all, the phonology and syntax of English, the role of mother tongue, welfare benefits, record keeping and evaluation. The aim is to create the awareness that having a language and a culture before one starts learning another language is a valuable asset rather than a disadvantage, and that the tutors should learn to draw and build upon it.

The centres are widely advertised through posters in English and various ethnic minority languages. They are displayed at various public places such as libraries, community centres, clinics, places of work, etc. The centres function for approximately 30 weeks a year and do not charge any fees. Since the curriculum is completely client-oriented, assessment and moving on to the next level are neither examination-dependent nor time-bound. The centres have considerable flexibility and dynamism in this respect. Whenever learners and their tutors feel that the learners have acquired a particular set of skills, they can proceed to the next appropriate level. In practice, however, most of the laudable objectives of the ESOL centres remain unattained because of a lack of funding, non-availability of teaching space and teaching materials, lack of motivation among some of the learners, a high drop-out rate at most centres, non-availability of full-time professional teachers and highly variable proficiency levels of the learners. Some of the centres which function satisfactorily have a highly competent and qualified teaching faculty, adequate teaching facilities, motivated learners and a very active participation in the life of the community. A few centres have introduced the system of teacher-appraisal to ensure that the students have received appropriate tuition and that the objectives of the scheme are being met. The tutors are supervised by the organisers periodically.

Country of origin

Table 4.1 shows the distribution of our informants by country of origin. The sample appears to represent most of the important migrant groups settled in Britain. The largest proportion, i.e. 84 out of 133, belongs to South Asia, which includes India, Pakistan and Bangladesh. The African ($n = 7$) and Middle Eastern countries ($n = 5$) are not so well represented. Twenty-four informants come from the Far East (China, Hong Kong, etc.), six from Europe and Latin America and seven from Iran.

Table 4.1 Country of origin of informants

South Asia		Far East (China & Others)		Europe and Latin America	
India	29	China	9	Spain	2
Pakistan	47	Hong Kong	6	Germany	1
Bangladesh	8	Vietnam	1	Portugal	1
		Singapore	1	Peru	2
		Taiwan	2		
		Korea	3		
		Japan	1		
		Malaysia	1		
Middle East		*Iran*		*Africa*	
Iraq	2	Iran	7	Sudan	2
Lebanon	1			Somalia	5
Turkey	2				

It is only from India and Pakistan that we have a substantial number of informants. Our observations about informants from other parts of the world should therefore be treated as highly tentative because of the small number of informants in each group.

Age and Sex-wise Distribution

Our sample consists largely of females and the greater proportion of informants (approximately 77%) are below 46 years of age. It is clear from Figure 4.1 that females outnumber males in each age group except that of the 36–45 year olds.

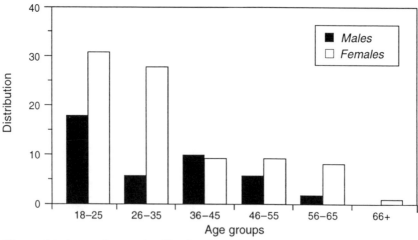

Figure 4.1 Age and sex-wise distribution of the sample

The first two age groups are of particular interest because here the number of males are extremely low. These two groups span the age range 18–35 years, which is the most productive age in terms of work and employment. As will be seen later, the majority of the females in these two age groups are unemployed.

Occupational Patterns

A substantial number of ESOL learners are either housewives (43%) or unemployed men (16%). Table 4.2 gives the details of the occupational status of our informants.

Table 4.2 Occupational patterns of ESOL learners

Occupation	% of sample	Occupation	% of sample
Housewives	42.62	Unskilled workers	3.28
Unemployed males	15.57	Professionals	3.28
Students	26.23	Businessmen	1.64
Skilled workers	7.38		

Most of the students in the sample are recent arrivals and attending ESOL classes to help them cope with their day-to-day interactions with the host society. The group of skilled workers include upholsterers, technicians, mechanics and tailors. The unskilled workers are generally manual labourers. Professionals, though highly educated, but not proficient in communicating in English, come to the ESOL classes with the hope of improving their communication skills.

Age at Arrival and Length of Stay

The present age of the informants (Mean = 32.75) is a function of their age at arrival (Mean = 27.17) and their length of stay in the UK (Mean = 6.08). Table 4.3 gives details of age at arrival and length of stay in the UK for the different groups of informants.

Table 4.3 Age at arrival and length of stay

Country of origin	Age at arrival (yrs)	Length of stay in the UK (yrs)
India	29.15	9.62
Pakistan	18.47	7.00
Far East	29.31	8.96
Europe	31.00	6.60
Bangladesh	20.00	6.71
Iran	31.21	4.28
Africa	22.13	1.13
Middle East	35.60	4.40

The Indian informants have lived in the UK the longest, whereas the African informants have, on an average, lived here for just over a year. This difference in length of stay, given that their average age at arrivals is not significantly different, may have important implications for both sociolinguistic stereotypes and language proficiency. In fact, in terms of age at arrival (except for the Pakistanis, who seem to have arrived rather young) the mean age at arrival of most groups is fairly close to the overall mean of 27 years.

Educational Background

Most of our informants have a fairly poor socioeconomic background. In most cases, their level of education is rather low and their use of English severely limited.

Family's Educational Level

The level of education of the informants' families in each group is shown in Table 4.4.

Table 4.4 Level of education of the informants and of their families

Country	Family	Own
India	34.66	43.18
Pakistan	22.14	37.23
Far East	43.05	60.40
Europe	50.00	55.55
Bangladesh	29.16	45.83
Iran	61.90	73.31
Africa	42.86	50.00
Middle East	46.66	66.66

The level of education of the families from Pakistan, Bangladesh and India is particularly low and stands in sharp contrast to the fairly high educational levels of families from Europe and Iran. A similar contrast is to be seen in the informants' own educational background as well. However, in all cases the informants' own educational level is higher than their family's. It is the informants from Iran, the Middle East and China who exhibit significantly high levels of personal education.

Claimed Control of English and Mother Tongue

Table 4.5 shows the average claimed proficiency in English and in the mother tongue for each of the groups involved in the study.

Table 4.5 Claimed control of English and in the mother tongue

Country	English	Mother tongue
India	46.03	81.25
Pakistan	57.32	67.03
Far East	56.11	91.32
Europe	61.11	98.61
Bangladesh	60.42	85.42
Iran	63.09	91.66
Africa	51.39	76.19
Middle East	63.89	85.41

The informants' self-rating of their proficiency in their mother tongue (Mean = 84.61%) is much higher than their assessment of their proficiency in English (Mean = 57.42%). This is also consistently true of each of the groups considered separately. It is of utmost importance that despite the prestige and power of English in the host as well as in the informants' own community, self-rating of mother tongue skills has not declined except in the case of informants from Pakistan (see Chapter 5 for more details).

Teachers' Evaluation, Claimed Control of English and Educational Background

Table 4.6 presents the scores for claimed control of English, level of education and teachers' evaluation and shows that all these dimensions of the learning situation are closely related.

Table 4.6 Informants' claimed control of English, their educational background and teachers' evaluation of their ESOL skills

Country of origin	Claimed control	Educational background	Teachers' evaluation
India	46.03	43.18	38.33
Pakistan	57.32	37.23	59.17
Far East	56.11	60.40	62.50
Europe	61.11	55.55	69.17
Bangladesh	60.42	45.83	67.50
Iran	63.09	73.81	69.04
Africa	51.39	50.00	57.14
Middle East	63.89	66.66	61.66

The informants from Iran clearly show that those who have a highly positive self-image of their abilities and a significantly good educational background are evaluated most favourably by the teachers. The informants from Pakistan and Bangladesh emphatically demonstrate that their positive self-image is far more important than going to a good school. The Indian informants clearly show that if one has a low self-image of one's target language (in this case English) abilities and a poor educational background, one is likely to be evaluated very unfavourably by the teachers.

Exposure to English through Radio and Television

Informants' exposure to the mass media is an important aspect of learning a second language. Table 4.7 shows the different groups' exposure to English through TV and radio.

Table 4.7 Exposure of English through TV and radio

Country	TV	Radio
India	71.43	55.36
Pakistan	73.86	34.78
Far East	69.56	47.91
Europe	66.66	41.66
Bangladesh	46.87	21.43
Iran	71.43	57.14
Africa	78.57	20.00
Middle East	90.00	60.00

The informants from Bangladesh clearly stand out. They receive the least exposure to English through the mass media. It would be interesting to examine what implications this limited exposure has for language proficiency. Unlike those from Bangladesh, the informants from the Middle East have the highest exposure to English through both radio and television. All the ESOL learners listen to the radio much less frequently than they watch the television. This may be because watching TV makes fewer demands on language skills than listening to the radio without visual aids.

Patterns of the Use of English in Different Domains

Figure 4.2 shows that while learning English in a formal classroom context our informants are also exposed to spontaneous, uncontrolled real life contexts in which they have to use the language in the process of living and interacting with the host community.

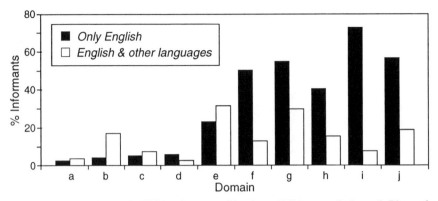

a: Writing letters home; b: Writing letters to friends; c: Talking to relatives; d: Place of worship; e: Talking to friends and neighbours; f: At the doctor's; g: Shopping; h: Work-mates; i: With boss at work; j: With public at work.

Figure 4.2 Use of English in different domains

It is, however, clear that except in the domains of shopping, going to the doctor, workmates, with boss at work, and with public at work where one has very little choice, ESOL learners generally use their native languages along with English in most domains of activity. The situations which the informants found most difficult to negotiate included reading newspapers and magazines, official letters and documents, instructions for the use of medicines and talking to government officials. But, in spite of this limited ability to use English, it is interesting to note that many informants claim to know English fairly well or indeed very well. However, this does not reflect their actual level of competence in spoken English.

Mother Tongue

Table 4.8 represents a comprehensive picture of the informants' use of the mother tongue with different interlocutors (both in and outside of home). This table clearly shows the predominance of the mother tongue in the domains of home, kinship network and friends among informants from all the countries represented in our study. The use of the mother tongue consistently declines as one moves outside into domains involving shopping, interaction with doctors, etc. Indeed, the domains of shopping and talking to doctors clearly belong to English. A high percentage of Indians, however, claim to use the mother tongue when talking to doctors; this may be attributed to the fact that a large number of medical practitioners in the UK are from the Indian subcontinent, and the ESOL learners may have registered with a doctor who could speak their mother tongue. The figures for the use of the mother tongue in the domain of religion are low not because the use of English is high, but because the religious domain naturally belongs to Classical Sanskrit, Arabic or Persian.

Table 4.8 Patterns of the use of the mother tongue in and outside the home

Country	Grand-parents	Parents	Husband/Wife	Brothers	Sisters	Children (>5)	Children (<5)	Talking to relatives (staying separately)	Writing letters to relatives (staying at a distance)	Talking to friends/neighbours	Writing letters to friends	Talking to doctors	Shopping	Religion
India (29)	100.00	90.48	88.00	76.47	72.22	68.42	76.19	100.00	95.83	37.93	75.00	66.66	11.54	34.48
Pakistan (47)	100.00	97.43	72.73	76.47	81.39	58.60	60.60	88.88	93.02	37.78	80.00	36.17	15.21	61.70
China & Others (24)	100.00	100.00	85.00	100.00	100.00	85.71	78.57	100.00	100.00	50.00	61.90	16.66	20.00	65.20
Europe (6)	100.00	100.00	40.00	100.00	100.00	20.00	33.33	88.88	100.00	00.00	50.00	16.66	00.00	33.30
Bangladesh (8)	—	87.50	66.66	40.00	33.33	66.66	100.00	87.50	87.50	12.50	87.50	25.00	12.50	37.50
Iran (7)	100.00	85.71	85.71	85.71	85.71	50.00	40.00	85.71	100.00	00.00	71.42	00.00	00.00	14.28
Africa (7)	100.00	83.33	100.00	75.00	66.66	40.00	40.00	66.00	71.43	71.43	71.42	00.00	00.00	14.28
Middle East (5)	100.00	100.00	66.66	100.00	100.00	50.00	—	66.66	66.66	00.00	75.00	00.00	00.00	40.00

Irrespective of the country of origin and the length of stay in the UK, all the informants largely use the mother tongue with their parents and grandparents. All the informants from China, Middle East and Europe use only mother tongue in interactions with grandparents, parents and siblings, whereas some from India, Pakistan, Iran and Africa also use English in such interactions. Those from Bangladesh (on whom we have limited data) do not reflect this pattern of mother tongue use among the siblings. The most striking feature of Table 4.8 is the rapidly decreasing number of informants who use the mother tongue with children.

This is the area of interaction which most strikingly separates the Asians from the Europeans, Africans and those from the Middle East. Informants from Europe, Iran, Africa and the Middle East do not use the mother tongue with their children to the same degree. The case of Bangladeshis is very interesting. Though most of them avoid using their mother tongue when talking with brothers and sisters and friends and neighbours, they seem to be very keen on using the mother tongue with children.

The desire to retain the mother tongue is further underlined by the data in Table 4.8. Most of the informants, irrespective of their country of origin, claim to have very high levels of proficiency in all the four skills in their mother tongue. Except for those from Africa and the Middle East, most parents wish their children to have mother tongue classes in schools. Even in the case of Africa and the Middle East, the lack of desire for retention should not be interpreted as a disregard for their mother tongue. Whereas the Asians have made sincere efforts on their own to organise mother tongue language teaching programmes, and many parents already send their children to such classes, government or voluntary help with organising classes in Persian, Arabic and various African languages has only recently taken off.

Linguistic Stereotypes

Our informants' linguistic stereotypes of English are presented in Figure 4.3. The picture here is consistent with the overall findings in Figure 4.2 and shows that the informants' use of English is primarily governed by pragmatic considerations or the need to use the language in order to live and advance their prospects in the new country. Not only do nearly 90% of the informants show a strongly positive evaluation of the target language – English – for its instrumental/achievement oriented trait of 'useful', but not a single person denies its usefulness. However, with regard to traits like 'sweet', 'scientific' and 'easy', only 41% or fewer of the informants show strongly positive attitude to the language.

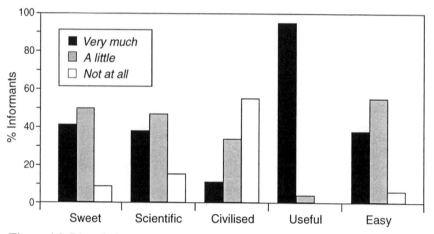

Figure 4.3 Linguistic stereotypes of English language

The picture is particularly disturbing in the case of English being 'civilised'. Fewer than 11% of the informants judge English to be highly 'civilised' ('very much') and over 55% deny its being 'civilised' at all. This is despite the fact that English enjoys a high prestige in the countries which were once dominated by Britain as colonial power and are now independent. This is also despite the fact that English has gained prestige in other countries with its emergence as a world language, and in Britain it is the language of access to all types of institutionalised authority and to social success. It could be that the association of English with past colonialism continues to be a part of their subconscious self.

Social Stereotypes

Figure 4.4 shows the informants' evaluation of 'the English people', 'of their own linguistic community' and 'the way you would like to be' in terms of such unipolar attributes as 'hardworking', 'helpful', 'efficient', etc. These evaluations further substantiate our findings that the informants consider the host society superior only in terms of the achievement-oriented attributes. (Our analysis is based only on the nine positive attributes. We have excluded the seven negative attributes because during our fieldwork we felt that the informants had difficulty in understanding as well as scaling these attributes.) Oller *et al.* (1977) had found that Chinese ESOL learners in the United States were not particularly integratively oriented towards the Americans. They tended to rate the Chinese higher on desirable personal traits such as 'kindness', 'friendliness', etc., while they appeared to be positively oriented towards the Americans with respect to such achievement-oriented traits as 'successfulness' and 'confidence'.

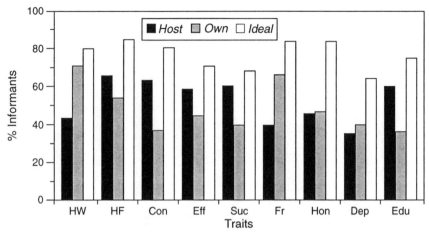

HW = Hardworking; HF = Helpful; Con = Confident; Eff = Efficient; Suc = Successful;
Fr = Friendly; Hon = Honest; Dep = Dependable; Edu = Educated.

Figure 4.4 Social stereotypes

Our study supports their findings: our ESOL learners, too, view the host society positively only on those attributes which have an achievement orientation, i.e. 'successful', 'educated', 'efficient' and 'confident'. But in terms of the more personal attributes such as 'hardworking', 'honest', 'dependable' and 'friendly', these learners rank their own community higher. Both the host society and the learners' own groups fall far short of the ideal, though.

In our earlier study (Khanna *et al.,* 1990) we had found that immigrants, on the whole, rate the host community higher on achievement-oriented attributes like 'educated', 'efficient' and 'successful', but they rate their own community higher on desirable personal traits such as 'hardworking', 'honest', 'dependable' and 'friendly'. Table 4.9 presents our informants' social stereotypes of the host and their own communities and it substantiates our earlier findings. Among the achievement-oriented attributes, most of the groups view the host community as more 'successful' than their own community. Only those from Iran and Africa regard both communities as equally 'successful'. With the exception of the Chinese and Iranians, most of the informants also rate the host community consistently higher than their own community for being 'efficient'. The case of the Iranians really stands out and does not fit the general pattern seen in Table 4.9. Except for the achievement-oriented attribute 'confident', the Iranians appear to view the host community negatively with respect to all the traits. It is difficult for us to explain this unique feature because it may have political and/or historical roots. All the other groups find the host community at least no less 'confident' than their own. In the case of the attribute 'educated', all the groups except those from Iran and the Middle East view the host community as more 'educated' than their own.

Table 4.9 Migrants' stereotypes of their own and the host community

Country		Stereotype								
		Hard-working	Helpful	Confident	Efficient	Successful	Friendly	Honest	Dependable	Educated
India (29)	Host	42	61	68	58	77	38	31	32	66
	Own	79	39	34	46	62	59	31	21	24
Pakistan (47)	Host	37	67	55	69	63	37	53	29	61
	Own	72	54	34	44	27	67	48	49	26
China & Others (24)	Host	22	61	52	33	39	55	35	43	52
	Own	67	50	29	38	32	46	46	30	33
Europe (6)	Host	33	50	67	67	67	33	67	17	83
	Own	83	67	67	33	0	100	33	50	67
Bangladesh (8)	Host	63	75	88	67	63	50	75	63	88
	Own	36	36	36	29	50	75	43	43	63
Iran (7)	Host	14	14	50	29	29	14	14	17	17
	Own	57	57	14	57	29	100	57	33	29
Africa (7)	Host	100	86	100	86	86	57	86	71	71
	Own	86	86	100	67	86	86	100	100	71
Middle East (5)	Host	75	75	75	75	67	50	50	33	33
	Own	60	60	25	50	50	67	60	67	50

The case of the Bangladeshis is exactly opposite to that of the Iranians. Whereas the Iranians consistently rate their own community more positively, the Bangladeshis consistently rate the host society more positively, irrespective of the attribute involved. Africans are midway between these two extremes, as their stereotypes of the host and their own community are hardly differentiated. As we have already pointed out, at least some of these observations must be treated as tentative because the size of the sample in some of the groups is very small. Of the remaining five groups, all except the informants from the Middle East regard their own community as more 'hardworking' than the host community; but all of them, except the Europeans, regard the host community as more 'helpful'. In general, one's own community is seen as more 'friendly', and 'dependable', though there are some exceptions.

Motivational Orientation

Following Gardner & Lambert's (1972) distinction between integrative and instrumental motivation, 10 statements were designed to elicit motivational orientation of the ESOL learners (see Chapter 2). The informants were asked to indicate on a 3-point scale how important each reason was for their learning English as a second language. The informants' motivational orientation for learning English (both integrative and instrumental) is presented in Figure 4.5.

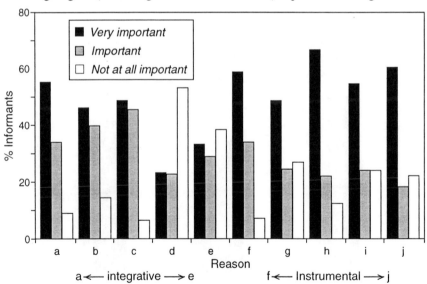

a: Understand English people; b: To gain friends; c: Interact with English people; d: Behave as the English; e: Study English literature; f: Become independent; g: Business; h: Get a good job; i: Get promotions; j: Acquire qualifications.

Figure 4.5 Motivational orientation

While only 23% of the informants consider that 'to think and behave as the English do' is a very important reason for learning English, nearly 67% of them regard getting 'a good job' as a very important reason for doing so. Besides being consistent with the earlier findings, this study confirms that pragmatic/instrumental considerations far outweigh the associative/integrative ones and accordingly determine the motivational orientation of the informants. Since success in Britain depends largely on understanding the British way of life and on interacting with the people, a substantial percentage of the informants consider these integrative reasons to be very important. However, the primary motivation for learning English is to get jobs and quick promotions, to acquire better qualifications and to become independent. For about 67% of the informants, 'behaving as one of the host society' or 'having an interest in English literature' do not appear to be very important reasons for learning English. Thus, even though the informants have been learning English in the UK, their motivational orientation cannot be characterised as an integrative one (*cf.* also Oller *et al.,* 1977). Instead, they learn the language because it helps them promote their well-being in this country, but they would not lose their ethnic identity in the process (Agnihotri, 1979).

Motivational Intensity

Our informants' motivation for learning English, then, is primarily instrumental and not integrative. However, as Figure 4.6 shows, their motivational intensity to learn the language in the classroom and to make the best use of the opportunities available to them is very strong. Most of them are very eager to participate in classroom interaction, do extra assignments and seek help from the teacher.

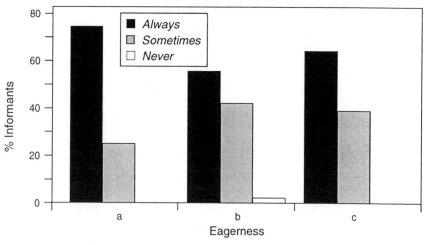

a: Answer questions; b: Do extra assignments; c: Seek help.

Figure 4.6 Motivational intensity

The strong desire to learn the language is particularly encouraging considering the odds most learners face when coming to ESOL classes. Bearing in mind that the majority of ESOL learners have been in Britain for less than five years, are unemployed men and women under the age of 45, and some of them have had a fairly good education, it would be reasonable to expect that they would want to learn English not only to improve their prospects in the job market, but also for their own general survival – especially if they wish to move out of the ethnic ghetto. In addition, over two-thirds of the learners are women who mostly come from countries with very strong family-centred sociocultural role-norms. These norms severely restrict them from going out alone and thus from learning the language through social interactions with members of the host community. They therefore depend on ESOL classes to learn the language. There are two issues that need to be addressed, namely: (a) why our informants' motivation to learn English is very strong even though their attitude to the English host community is only moderately positive; and (b) why this motivation is instrumentally rather than integratively oriented. The sociopolitical ideological considerations which have determined the kind, quality and volume of immigrants arriving in post-World War II Britain, as well as their relationship with the host community, including that of their ethnic and linguistic identity (from 'assimilation' to integration' to 'equality of opportunity' within a multiracial/cultural/lingual society) may well play a role in explaining these questions.

5 Sociolinguistic Correlates of Proficiency in English

Introduction

The analysis of our data is centred around three major issues: (a) nature of relationship between different social psychological variables and language proficiency as seen through teachers' evaluation; (b) the extent of the informants' retention of mother tongue in relation to the length of their stay in UK; and (c) the nature of relationship between linguistic stereotypes and language proficiency.

Correlational and Regression Analysis

Twenty-seven variables relating to the personal, social-psychological and language proficiency aspects of the informants were created for correlational and regression analysis. The correlation of these variables is shown in Table 5.1.

The variables shown in Table 5.2 correlate significantly with the informants' proficiency assessed by their teachers.

The variables relating to the personal and social background of the learners correlate significantly with the teachers' evaluation of learners' level of proficiency in English. Age correlates negatively with the grades given by the teachers, suggesting that the higher the age of the learners the lower the level of their proficiency. As pointed out earlier, the fact that the younger informants' level of proficiency is rated higher than the older ones may appear rather surprising in the context of the fact that the younger ones are, generally speaking, relatively recent arrivals while the older ones have been in Britain much longer. However, when we examine this question in the context of the history and patterns of immigration into Britain and note that the illiterate or semi-educated adults – the older group – who arrived in the UK to work in shifts in the man-power starved British industries, lived in ethnic shelters and had little incentive or pressure to learn English, nor did there exist then the kind of opportunities to learn English that exist now. Most of the bachelor migrants who came through chain migrations were content to learn just about enough to get along in their manual jobs, spending all their leisure hours among their own people in the crowded bachelor bedsits.

Table 5.1 Correlation matrix

Variables	1	2	3	4	5	6	7	8	9	10	11	12	13	14	15	16	17	18	19	20	21	22	23	24	25	26	27
1. Sex		02	-16	-25	37	13	12	24	08	-16	-05	13	-04	00	01	-19	03	-12	-00	07	-08	05	-37	03	14	01	-04
2. Age			-04	50	23	-26	-38	-20	-41	-12	-28	-15	-14	-07	-08	07	-01	-04	-20	-13	-23	07	-33	-24	-02	-06	-27
3. Occupation				-13	14	31	-14	07	-02	11	-06	17	14	-01	11	21	-11	-01	18	25	14	-14	10	04	29	29	06
4. No. of years in UK					-19	-59	-17	07	-24	-11	02	00	10	09	-07	14	-09	12	-16	-07	-11	07	03	-15	-05	-22	-07
5. Education of family						41	11	-28	-09	-05	02	11	07	-04	05	-04	-10	-16	15	13	06	17	-24	06	29	32	-04
6. Education of self							14	37	26	20	-09	17	16	02	28	13	08	-14	25	36	02	18	03	07	24	38	34
7. Parents' English skills								12	23	-11	32	24	22	04	08	-03	-15	-13	15	08	23	21	19	14	14	08	20
8. Mother tongue skills									29	07	07	25	12	19	23	04	07	-16	17	22	17	11	-02	07	10	18	16
9. English skills (self-rating)										25	29	30	37	04	15	07	-12	09	06	24	14	12	14	02	04	12	58
10. Frequency of use of English at home											34	35	25	12	25	12	-09	03	19	06	09	19	02	06	25	25	23
11. English at home with different people												35	23	08	23	01	-20	17	24	06	09	09	07	05	01	02	19
12. Patterns of language													33	17	14	25	-21	-12	23	23	13	15	-09	10	12	15	24
13. Ease in using English														25	19	12	06	01	15	19	17	07	13	05	-08	13	27
14. English TV															39	14	15	02	07	-06	02	24	19	-13	-09	-11	23
15. English radio																36	11	11	18	14	03	23	03	-20	09	03	27
16. English at work																	04	-06	05	-03	10	33	31	09	01	01	34
17. Desire to improve English skills																		03	-05	-02	08	16	05	-11	-23	-08	02
18. Desire to improve MT skills																			11	-17	-12	-14	06	-15	-15	-25	10
19. Attitude to English																				28	09	03	17	25	12	23	17
20. Desire to learn English																					15	04	09	28	14	39	31
21. Motivational intensity																						11	27	20	-03	15	05
22. Integrative motivation																							30	03	15	04	33
23. Instrumental motivation																								01	-11	-16	45
24. Stereotypes of the British																									29	38	-08
25. Stereotypes of the self																										39	05
26. Stereotypes of the ideal																											03
27. Teachers' evaluation																											—

** Highly significant; * Significant

Table 5.2 Variables correlating significantly with teachers' evaluation (V. 27)

Variable No.	Variable	Correlation coefficient
2	Age	−0.27* (n = 129)
6	Education of the self	0.34** (n = 132)
9	Self-rating of English skills	0.58** (n = 98)
10	Frequency of English at home	0.23 (n = 74)
12	Patterns of language use	0.24* (n = 133)
13	Ease in the use of English	0.27* (n = 132)
14	Exposure to English (TV)	0.23 (n = 128)
15	Exposure to English (Radio)	0.27* (n = 126)
16	Use of English at work	0.34* (n = 105)
17	Desire to learn English	0.31** (n = 133)
22	Integrative motivation	0.33** (n = 132)
23	Instrumental motivation	0.45** (n = 133)

** Highly significant
* Significant

Two variables which have highly significant correlations with the teachers' evaluation are the informants' level of education and their self-rating of English skills. It appears that if an ESOL learner has good educational background and a positive image of his abilities in English, his proficiency level is likely to be high.

The next set of social variables which are significant concern informants' patterns of language use and their exposure to English in different domains of activity. The informants' level of proficiency in English varies directly with their use of English at work and at other places outside the home. Similarly, the greater is the degree of English used at work and at other places outside home, the greater is the degree of proficiency achieved. Similarly, the greater the degree of exposure to English through radio and TV, the higher is the level of proficiency achieved. It is interesting to note that self-rating in English skills is strongly correlated with all the patterns of language use and exposure variables. It is also strongly correlated with the desire to learn English. The overwhelming importance of the language use/language exposure variables that we have found in our studies in India is further reiterated in this study too.

When we turn to the social psychological variables we notice that the informants' attitude towards English, motivational intensity and social stereotypes do not show any significant correlation with teachers' ratings of the informants' level of proficiency. The most important variables include their desire to learn English and instrumental and integrative motivation. Despite the fact that English is being learnt in a context where the target language community constitutes the majority group, it is the instrumental rather than the integrative motivation which shows a higher correlation with the proficiency levels of the informants. It would appear that the migrant groups would like to learn the language of the host society without at the same time losing their identity.

Though the attitudes and stereotypes of the informants do not contribute directly to the language proficiency, they seem to make important contributions to it indirectly as they often significantly correlate with the variables which bear significant correlations with the levels of proficiency. For example, the desire to learn English which correlates significantly with the proficiency ($r =$ 0.31**) also correlates significantly with the attitude towards English, stereotypes of the English people and stereotypes of an ideal community. None of these three variables, considered separately, shows any significant correlation with proficiency. This configuration of the desire to learn English, positive attitude to the target language and the target language community, is indeed significant.

Unlike the study of Gardner & Lambert (1972), motivational variables in our study do not correlate with attitudinal variables. They correlate significantly with such variables as patterns of language use, exposure to English and motivational intensity.

If we examine the situation of ESOL learners in Britain in the context of Klein's (1986) dimensions of second language acquisition, we may conclude that these learners are ideally placed for learning English. Their immediate communicative needs and not the integrative outlook constitute the basis of their propensity to learn English: they have considerable access to English in both spontaneous and tutored language settings: they have a very strong desire to use English in as many contexts as possible. It is therefore not surprising that despite their impoverished English background, the average score for the total population by the teachers was above 64%. It is also clear that the basis for their strong desire is not so much to become like the British but to have greater exposure to English and to use it in as many contexts as possible to meet their communicative needs. Our position in this respect is slightly, though not insignificantly, different from the one held by Gardner, Lambert and their associates. They tried to show that an integrative outlook contributed significantly to language proficiency and that a cluster of positive attitudes to the target language and the target language group constituted the basis of this motivational orientation. Our study shows that the instrumental cluster of variables which constitutes the basis of this propensity is not attitudinal but social. Those who have a stronger communicative need do better and look for greater opportunities for using English. Such learners also evaluate their skills in English very highly. The step-wise multiple regression in Table 5.3 shows that this self-esteem with regard to control over English accounts for 35% variance in the scores given by the teachers. The other two important predictor variables are age and patterns of language use. As already pointed out, age in this context does not only mean that the younger you are the better the level of your proficiency. It also subsumes at what point in the history of migration you migrated.

Those who came with the intention of staying for a few years and returning home with some money did not make any special efforts to interact with the native speakers; but those who came with the *fait accompli* of becoming a member of a minority group which was more or less well entrenched in the British society, availed themselves of every possible opportunity to learn English. It therefore seems consistent with our analysis that 10% of the variance should be contributed by the patterns of language use.

Table 5.3 Stepwise multiple regression with teachers' evaluation as the dependent variable

Step	Variable	Multiple	R R square	R SQ change
1	Self-rating of English	0.59	0.35	0.35
2	Age	0.68	0.46	0.11
3	Patterns of language use	0.75	0.56	0.10

Length of Stay and Retention of the Mother Tongue

As we noticed above, age correlates negatively with proficiency in English. In fact, in the case of immigrants age is really a function of age at arrival and length of stay. It is not necessarily the case that people who are older have also stayed longer in England. We tried to examine the issue of length of stay in some detail.

Since we had a substantial number of informants from India and Pakistan we decided to concentrate on these two groups only. The sample from India and Pakistan was divided into three groups:

Group	Length of stay in UK
A	Less than 3 years
B	Between 4 and 7 years
C	Eight or more years

Figure 5.1 shows how strongly immigrants are motivated to plan strategies for maintaining their mother tongue.

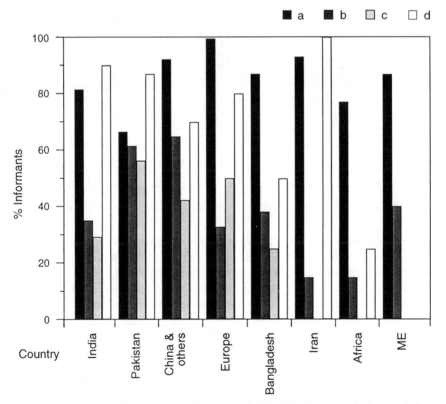

a: Average claimed proficiency in mother tongue; b: No. of informants who have a desire to improve their mother tongue; c: No. of parents sending children to mother tongue classes in community centres; d: No. of parents wanting schools to provide lessons in the mother tongue.

Figure 5.1 Migrants' claimed proficiency in their mother tongue and the strategies of maintaining them

Almost all groups send their children to the mother tongue classes and most of them wish that the school would provide adequate facilities for the teaching of their mother tongues. The strongest evidence for the retention of mother tongue is seen in Figures 5.2 and 5.3. Figure 5.2 shows the use of mother tongue in the domains of home and outside the home, in relation to the length of stay in the UK.

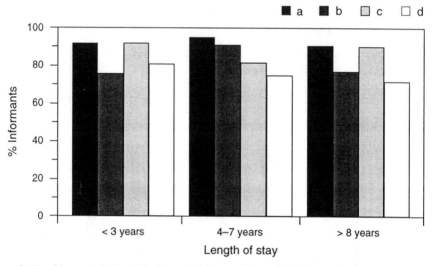

a: India – Home; b: India – Outside; c: Pakistan – Home; d: Pakistan – Outside.

Figure 5.2 Length of stay and the use of mother tongue at home and outside

We expected the claimed use of the mother tongue to be inversely proportional to the length of stay in the UK. Figure 5.2 contradicts this hypothesis most emphatically. Irrespective of whether the stay is less than 3 years (Group a), between 4 and 7 years (Group b) or 8 or more years (Group c), the use of the mother tongue remains above 90% in the domain of home for both Indians and Pakistanis. Even in the outside domain we notice a substantial use of the mother tongue in the case of both Indians and Pakistanis. Again, as it can be seen in Figure 5.3, though both in the case of Indians and Pakistanis there is a decline in claimed proficiency in the mother tongue, its image is still significantly positive. The correlation between the length of stay in the UK and education was highly significant, though negative ($r = -0.59, p < 0.001$). It suggests that the people who migrated early were not always well-educated. It is, therefore, not surprising that those with longer stay evaluate their control of the mother tongue less positively than those who have come more recently. This was a natural consequence of most of the early migrants lacking in literacy skills in their mother tongue.

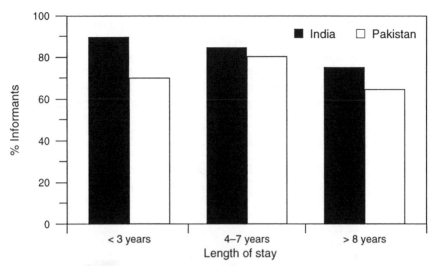

Figure 5.3 Length of stay and claimed proficiency in the mother tongue

Figure 5.4 shows the changes in the stereotypes of the host and own community in relation to the length of stay in the UK. Once again, we notice parallel developments in the case of India and Pakistan. In the case of the host society's image there is a decline in the immigrants' estimate of the host society. The image of one's own community does not change substantially, though in the case of Pakistan there is a visible improvement.

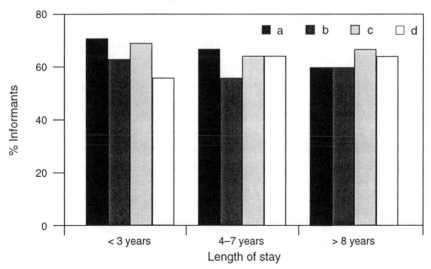

a: India – Host; b: India – Own; c: Pakistan – Host; d: Pakistan – Own.

Figure 5.4 Length of stay and stereotypes of the host and own community

It is in Figure 5.5 that Indians and Pakistanis are distinguished sharply. The Pakistanis across different lengths of stay show a very strong desire to improve the knowledge of their mother tongue. However, as is clear from Figure 5.3, the desire to improve the mother tongue seems to be inversely proportionate to the claimed proficiency. Be that as it may, Figure 5.5 clearly shows the desire to acquire greater proficiency in the mother tongue with the increase in their length of stay.

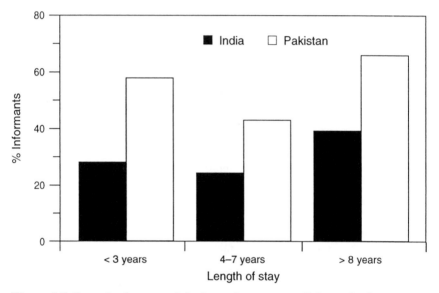

Figure 5.5 Length of stay and desire to improve proficiency in the mother tongue

It is clear from this discussion that irrespective of striking disparities between geographical, socioeconomic, political and cultural backgrounds, all the groups show a very strong desire to retain their mother tongues and use them in a variety of situations, in both home and outside domains. A detailed study of India and Pakistan shows that the length of stay does not subtract anything from this desire. The fact that there is a noticeable decline in the image of the host society as the length of stay increases is indeed worrying.

Linguistic Stereotypes and Language Proficiency

As already pointed out in Chapter 3, we designed a questionnaire to elicit the social and linguistic stereotypes of the informants. Logically speaking, the positive and negative values of social and linguistic stereotypes give us four quadrants, as in Figure 5.6.

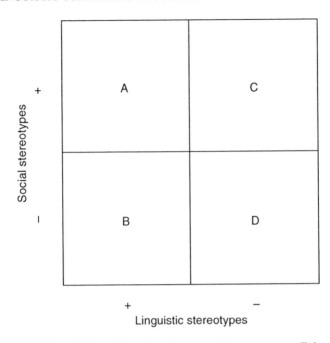

Figure 5.6 Social and linguistic stereotypes and language proficiency

On the basis of this figure we could use these combinations to formulate a very bold hypothesis providing a basis for a rich empirical investigation: communities in quadrant A where both the social and linguistic stereotypes are positive, may achieve the highest levels of proficiency in a second language. It is an area characterised by an integrative outlook towards the target language and the target language group. Diametrically opposed to quadrant A is quadrant D where both the social and linguistic stereotypes are negative. We would expect that communities with the lowest levels of proficiency would fall in this quadrant. The proficiency levels of the communities in quadrant B and C should be in-between those of communities in quadrants A and D because in the case of B only linguistic stereotypes are positive and in the case of C only social stereotypes are positive. What follows is a discussion of the proficiency levels in English of adult ESOL learners from six different migrant communities in Britain in terms of the above hypothesis.

The mean percentage of informants for the achievement-oriented stereotypes is approximately 60% or above for all the immigrant groups except the Chinese group. All the migrant communities evaluate the British people positively on social success stereotypes except the Chinese group (see Table 5.4).

Table 5.4 Stereotypes of British people among the migrant groups in Britain and language proficiency (achievement stereotypes) (% informants)

	Hard working	Con-fident	Efficient	Suc-cessful	Educated	Mean	Average score (out of 12)
Bangladeshi	63	88	67	63	88	74	8.1
African & Middle Eastern	61	76	61	55	41	59	7.9
European & Latin American	33	67	67	67	83	63	8.3
Chinese & others	22	52	33	39	52	40	7.5
Pakistani	37	55	69	63	61	57	7.1
Indian	42	68	58	77	66	62	4.6

But the mean percentage of informants for personal stereotypes is far lower than those for achievement-oriented stereotypes (see Table 5.5). Bangladeshis really stand out as the most integratively oriented towards the host society.

Table 5.5 Stereotypes of British people among the migrant groups in Britain and language proficiency (personal stereotypes) (% informants)

	Helpful	Friendly	Honest	Dependable	Mean	Average score (out of 12)
Bangladeshi	75	50	75	63	66	8.1
African & Middle Eastern	56	37	47	41	45	7.9
European & Latin American	50	33	67	17	42	8.3
Chinese & others	61	55	35	43	49	7.5
Pakistani	67	37	53	29	47	7.1
Indian	61	38	31	32	41	4.6

The stereotypes of the English language were measured in terms of the following five attributes: Useful, Difficult, Sweet, Scientific and Civilised. There were no significant differences among the different groups in the case of the first two attributes of *useful* and *difficult*. All the groups felt that English was a useful language and was easy to learn. There was a considerable variation across the different migrant groups in terms of the remaining three attributes (see Table 5.6).

Table 5.6 Stereotypes of English language among the migrant groups in Britain and their language proficiency (% informants)

	Sweet	Scientific	Civilised	Mean	Average score (out of 12)
Bangladeshi	57	29	83	56	8.1
African & Middle Eastern	65	67	57	63	7.9
European & Latin American	50	75	75	67	8.3
Chinese & others	67	50	83	67	7.5
Pakistani	28	31	47	35	7.1
Indian	18	20	36	25	4.6

On the basis of Tables 5.5 and 5.6, we may place the six immigrant groups in our study in the different quadrants of Figure 5.7.

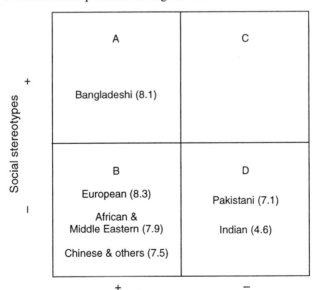

Figure 5.7 Informants' social & linguistic stereotypes and language proficiency

The only group which has clearly positive stereotypes of both the English language and the British people and falls in quadrant A is the Bangladeshi group. In terms of language proficiency it is next to the Europeans. Without underestimating the overwhelming importance of the social variables such as the length of stay and exposure, the case of the Bangladeshis shows that positive stereotypes of the target language and the target language group are strongly associated with the proficiency in the target language. It is interesting that the Indians, the Pakistanis and the Bangladeshis, who come from the same subcontinent, should be placed in diametrically opposed quadrants. Both the Indians and the Pakistanis have relatively negative stereotypes of both the target language and the target language group, though in terms of proficiency the Pakistanis are closer to the Bangladeshis. This is indeed a very complex feature. In quadrant B, which is characterised by positive linguistic stereotypes but negative social stereotypes, we have the Europeans, immigrants from Africa and the Middle East, China and others. It shows that high proficiency levels can be achieved without having an integrative outlook. It may be sufficient to have a positive attitude to the target language. The vacant quadrant C suggests that the groups which think positively of the target language groups but negatively of the target language are rare.

Most of our earlier studies (for example, Agnihotri *et al.*, 1988; Khanna, 1983; Khanna & Agnihotri, 1982, 1984) done in India showed that attitudinal variables did not play any significant role in second language acquisition. The present study conducted in the native language context suggests that the role of attitudinal variables is context-sensitive, and that in addition to the overwhelmingly important social variables, integrative outlook and a positive image of the target language group may be important factors. As one can see from Figure 5.7, the Bangladeshis are most integratively oriented and have high levels of language proficiency. In our interviews we felt that there was a strong feeling of insecurity among Bangladeshis and they had a very potent threat of racial discrimination. Since this sample is very small, further research is required to draw any valid conclusion or explanation.

China has a very long history of resisting Anglicisation and Westernisation; on the other hand recent changes in China have brought out the importance of learning English. They, therefore, have positive stereotypes of the English language but not of the British people. India, Pakistan, Africa and the Middle East share a similar history of colonial exploitation, yet people from India and Pakistan differ from Africa and the Middle East in having negative stereotypes of the British people. The growth of the national movement, as India became disillusioned with the glamour of Westernisation, was helped by the fact that it had a very rich historical past to turn to. It is only recently that the African people have had the opportunity to obtain access to their rich heritage.

Though the above discussion brings out the close relationship between stereotypes and language proficiency, it still leaves us with many intriguing questions: how do the Pakistanis, who have neither a positive image of English language nor a positive stereotype of the English people, achieve proficiency levels comparable to any other group with positive stereotypes? It is difficult to make any generalisation for migrants from Europe and Latin America because the sample size is extremely small.

The case of the Bangladeshis proves the widely accepted hypothesis outlined in the beginning remarkably well. It reconfirms the intuitively satisfying and generally held belief that positive social and linguistic stereotypes are associated with success in learning a second language. However, the case of the people from China, Africa and the Middle East shows that for the migrant groups it may be far more important to have positive stereotypes of the target language rather than of the target language group. But the Pakistanis, who share their linguistic and social stereotypes with the Indians, have very high levels of proficiency in English. This suggests that success in second language learning is not simply a question of having positive or negative social and linguistic stereotypes.

In order to explain this apparent anomaly as to why the Indians and the Pakistanis, though sharing negative social and linguistic stereotypes, had such different levels of proficiency, we examined other social and psychological variables. We found that the two communities showed no significant difference in terms of their mean age and mean length of stay in Britain. However, when we looked at their age at arrival in Britain we found a tenable explanation for the differences in the levels of their proficiency in English. The mean age of arrival in the case of the Pakistanis was 15 years, that as they had arrived at a relatively young age when potential for modifying linguistic habits is greater. The Indians, on the other hand, were twice as old when they arrived in Britain. Age at arrival thus appears to be a more important variable than social and linguistic stereotypes.

6 ESOL Teachers Speak

Introduction

As already pointed out (Chapter 2), we interviewed 30 ESOL teachers and administrators in Britain to elicit their views regarding the current status and future prospects of ESOL teaching in Britain. We had detailed discussions with the informants regarding the materials and methods being used in different ESOL centres, attitudes and motivation of their learners, role of the state and the immigrant communities, strategies the teachers used to evaluate the proficiency of the learners, and their present and future roles. Since ESOL was until recently not a mainstream activity in Britain and the infrastructural facilities available were meagre, teachers played a far more important role in the process of implementing ESOL programmes than they might normally do. With FEFC funding, ESOL appears to have become a mainstream activity and one hopes that corresponding changes in teaching methodology, materials and teaching aids will follow.

Status of ESOL

Although proficiency in English is a necessary requirement for both educational advancement and occupational mobility, ESOL has not received until recently the attention that is due to it. Not only that, there has hardly been any effort in the ESOL project to assess the total educational needs of the learners and relate the teaching of English to the skills and knowledge that the learners already have and to their overall development. During his field work in 1974, Agnihotri (1979, 1987) noted that an adult immigrant could learn English either through the evening classes organised by the LEAs or through the home-tutorship scheme arranged by the local Community Relations Office. Both these schemes failed miserably because of lack of resources and poor response. Agnihotri (1987: 58) reports the perceptions of a home-tutor who felt that the scheme was far too loosely organised and that the primary purpose of the scheme was not so much to teach English as to expose the learners to the culture of the host society. In our present survey also, both the non-native (black and European) and native teachers were unanimous in their assessment of the status of ESOL in Britain: 'ESL enjoys poor status. It is considered to be a low-level activity. Just social conversation. Not real language teaching.'

Most teachers felt that the funds and resources available for ESOL were highly inadequate. The multilingual and multicultural nature of the classrooms and the lack of adequate resources made very challenging demands on the teachers. There was no dearth of students; nor did the teachers or learners lack in motivation. What was really required was allocation of more funds and resources. In fact, the ESOL centres were housed in a variety of buildings ranging from dilapidated structures and Portacabins to very modern and well-equipped buildings. Some had substantial sums to maintain their existing infrastructural facilities and even to buy more equipment while others could barely survive. One ESOL teacher remarked:

> It was a school site ... when it was found unsafe we were given one day's notice to close our centre, so we agreed that our Portacabin should be back on the site ... We were told that it would be a temporary arrangement.... Two weeks ago we learnt that our Portacabin could stay on the site....

It is clear that the teachers felt that the state should examine the whole issue of ESOL teaching carefully and allocate more resources for its growth. In their opinion, if the status of ESOL continued declining, there would be very little hope that the already disadvantaged and marginalised minority groups would be able to get any benefit from them. As one of the active ESOL practitioners points out, ESOL as distinguished from EFL has always been a distinct pedagogical activity; ESOL is essentially a community-based programme where the needs of the learner range from literacy to basic education, and in some cases even to higher education. Even though there is substantial referral work between ESOL and EFL departments, the ESOL agenda remains significantly different from EFL. According to an ESOL professional:

> For me the practical differentiation is that the EFL staff are working for different accreditation. They are working towards the Cambridge certificate which is of value if you are going back to your country of origin. We are working towards accreditation which will get people permanent in this country. The EFL route is a fast track route not particularly suitable for ESOL learners who would like not only to learn English but also become familiar with sociocultural aspects of the British society. ESOL tends to take a functional rather than an ESP or topic based approach.

Institutional Racism and ESOL

Most teachers felt that ESOL was undermined by institutional racism and that this phenomenon will persist unless the state helped ESOL to become a mainstream activity. In fact, the continuous neglect and marginalisation of ESOL teaching activities was considered to be an example of racism and discrimination.

A number of ESOL practitioners and teacher trainers have in the past commented on the institutional racism prevalent in ESOL. For some, the very term ESOL implied a monolingual tradition with all its racist overtones. The Department of Education and Science (DES) now called Department of Further Education (DFE) has not been able to get rid of its assimilationist bias. Our understanding of the perceptions of ESOL teachers about racism are also corroborated by the research conducted by ALBSU (1989):

> The primary aim of provisions was to help the assimilation and integration of recent immigrants many of whom did not speak English and often the teaching approaches were based on the teaching of English to foreign students either in the UK or overseas ... much of it had little bearing on the lives of the people involved in ESOL.

About ESOL Centres and Classes

As already pointed out, there has been no uniform policy on the provisions available at ESOL centres in Great Britain. There were some centres which had more funds and more professional help available while other centres suffered from serious neglect. To quote from ALBSU (1989): Much ... was relatively unplanned and uncoordinated and the provision which did exist was patchy and of varying quality in different parts of England and Wales.

The courses at these centres could vary from 'English and keep fit classes' to 'ESOL and Sewing Classes'. Table 6.1 is an index of the enormous amount of random heterogeneity that existed at the ESOL centres. Some centres were over 50 years old, while some had been established very recently. The number of teachers at these centres could vary from 1 to 49. Some centres established in the 1970s were still managing their work with 1 to 5 teachers. Most of the ESOL centres fortunately did not charge their students any fees. Some just took token money for registration or photocopying. Some functioned twice a week only, while others worked for all the seven days in a week. Some had classes only in the morning, others in the morning and the evening, while still others had them thrice a day in the morning, evening and the afternoon. The most striking aspect of these classes was the multilingual nature of the classroom. The number of languages represented in any one centre could vary from 4 to 40. None of the ESOL centres was mono-lingual. This one feature alone was sufficient to warrant completely new planning for ESOL teaching. There was no doubt that each centre would be sensitive to its local environment and would plan its courses and teaching schedules according to the needs and convenience of its learners. Yet the heterogeneous character of the clientele, their disadvantaged status as minority groups and the lack of trained personnel in multilingual and multicultural education demanded a fresh look at the recruitment policy, infrastructural facilities and curriculum for the ESOL centres.

Table 6.1 Heterogeneous nature of the ESOL Centres

Centre	Year	Teachers	Fee	Days	Hours	M/E/A*	Students	Languages
A	1965	8	Free	5	1.5	M,E	12	4
B	1982	8	Free	1	1	M	17	5
C	—	—	Free	3	2	M	15	10
D	1940	8	5p	4	2	M,E,A	20	4
E	1977	1	50p	2	2	E,A	20	20
F	1974	49	Free	7	2.5	M,E	16	—
G	1980	5	Free	4	2.5	M,E	15	6
H	—	1	25p	4	2	M,E	14	13
I	1970	5	£3	4	2	M,E,A	13	12
J	1970	1	Free	4	2	M	12	5
K	1979	28	Free	5	1.5	M,E	10	6

*M = morning; E = evening; A = afternoon

Although a large number of students initially registered for courses at any given ESOL centre, their attendance in these classes fluctuated considerably during any course. It was dependent on many sociocultural and socioeconomic variables like, for example, structure of the family, the position of the learner in the family and his/her commitments to the family, and availability of creche facilities, the gender of the teacher, etc. One teacher said: When the weather is fine you could almost predict that the attendance in the class will be optimal,and most women will come well-dressed, looking very happy.

It is clear that many women regarded these classes as suitable and welcome occasions for social get-togethers. They made special efforts to be at the centre. We felt that it required a special kind of professional expertise to convert this motivation into a specific learning experience.

The attendance was also influenced by the age and gender of the learners. In particular in the South Asian communities, older women found it difficult to overcome their inhibitions to freely interact with the teachers, particularly if they were white males.

ESOL Teachers: Monolingual or Bilingual

One of the issues we wished to examine was whether the ESOL students were happy with mono- or bilingual teachers. What were the views of the ESOL teachers about this issue? Both the monolingual and bilingual teachers in general felt that the presence of a bilingual teacher, particularly in the early stages of teaching, certainly facilitated the learning process and helped the learners to overcome their initial hesitations. The very presence of bilingual teachers irrespective of whether they were familiar with the language and culture of the learners generated enormous amount of confidence among the learners and enhanced their motivation. One ESOL teacher commented:

> With the beginners, with Levels I, II and III, you have got to have a bilingual approach ... you can confuse the students if you were just using a language which he or she is not aware of ... you can depress them ... you could see their faces.... We don't realise, but when we put ourselves in their position, then we actually know.

And yet the Local Educational Authorities (LEAs) did not respond to this need. That the multilingual and multicultural ESOL class could learn with bilingual teachers has consistently been ignored. Most of the ESOL teachers are monolinguals, who seldom share the language of the learners. The need for having bilingual teachers should not be interpreted as a suggestion for teaching English through the mother tongue. On the contrary, familiarity with learners' language and culture may help the bilingual ESOL teachers to plan their lessons and activities better. An ESOL teacher said:

> Bilingual teaching does not mean you conduct the whole class in Gujrati or Urdu.... I don't want to use my mother tongue in ESOL classes. But sometimes when they are struggling or they are not clear about something, a word in the mother tongue is very helpful.... In English, there is a lot to explain.

However, both the teachers and the learners felt that at the higher levels, the mother tongue should be used sparingly. One teacher said: 'The advance group wants an English teacher.... They think that it is only the English teacher who can teach them English ... but with the beginners Level I and Level II students there could be a problem.'

In fact the multilingual ESOL classroom provided several opportunities for a variety of meaningful interactions. Many white teachers who did not share the languages and cultures of their students often encouraged the learners to help one another through the use of their native languages. One of them said: 'There are about 16 languages in a class and I could not speak all the languages even if I wanted to.... Yet I always have a feeling of handicap ... but I encouraged students to help each other using their mother tongues.'

Some teachers did have some misgivings about hiring bilingual teachers for the ESOL classes. They felt that there was perhaps some disadvantage in having bilingual teachers who shared the mother tongues of their students. One such teacher said:

> If they were dealing with a teacher who does not know their mother tongue, their motivation may be much more because they are trying to learn anyway,

whereas in the case of the bilingual teacher they may not make serious attempts to learn the target language.

Yet the number of such teachers was rather low. Most teachers, whether non-native or native, monolingual or bilingual, felt that the multilingual ESOL classroom did require a bilingual teacher and that such a classroom provided ideal conditions for a creative and meaningful cultural exchange. It does confirm the principle that in the act of teaching–learning, the teacher has as much to learn as the student. The relevance of having non-white bilingual teachers has begun to be appreciated now because multilingualism is perceived as a rich resource.

ESOL Learners

What the ESOL teachers found most striking about their students was their bewildering variety, not only in terms of their cultural and linguistic backgrounds but also in terms of their levels of proficiency in English. Most teachers felt that though it was obvious that most of the ESOL learners had come to Britain for economic prosperity, and that they would perhaps willingly assimilate those aspects of the British ways of life which were necessary for achieving that end, they certainly resented any threat to their native identity. Teachers felt that these adult men and women wanted to learn English for a variety of objectives, e.g. employment, higher education, effective participation in such encounters as talking to a doctor or hair dresser, shopping, counselling, seeking career information or medical help, etc. They may also need it to keep track of what their children were doing in general and in education in particular. Most teachers felt that it would be necessary to draw a profile of the communicative needs of the ESOL learners which might constitute the overall framework in which situation-specific materials and methods could be evolved.

We asked our teacher informants about the personality traits, motivation and learning strategies of their students. Though the variety of paths learners adopted to learn English was bewildering, a strong motivation to communicate and share experiences seemed to be the strongest motivation to learn. One teacher said:

> You ask me how do they learn? It is truly amazing. Some individuals just have such a personality. This woman from Vietnam.... She has never been to school. She was always left in charge of a young brother and several sisters while her parents worked in a village. Not one word of anything, no literacy skills. But she is learning, learning English perfectly well, determinedly, listening to the radio which she does not understand ... and she is learning.... I really don't know how.

The deep-seated desire to share messages and experience even when the language structure is not fully mastered may be the most important driving force behind accelerated second language acquisition. Though Krashen's (1982) principle of 'comprehensible input in anxiety free situations' has had considerable influence on second language acquisition theory and practice, the practical experience of teachers has always emphasised the importance of rich exposure, whether fully comprehensible or not, particularly in moments of crisis. Another teacher said about one of her students:

> I'm really struck by her progress. I think it has a lot to do with one's personality. Also the desperate need to communicate, you know, she has young children, she has been into the hospital to have children ... she may be forced to communicate in English. She can of course always find bilingual interpreters.... I think she is really an extrovert....

The Question of Gender

Our discussions with the teachers revealed that the gender of the ESOL teacher could be an important issue. Some of the teachers said that the South Asian Muslim women strongly resented the presence of a male teacher in the classroom. One of them said:

> Some of our women students reject men teachers ... male students do not have that attitude ... they accept female teachers ... but Muslim women students are not supposed to talk to any stranger male with whom they do not have a relationship ... it is purely religious ... once we had a male teacher to come and help us, the women students immediately dropped out ... there was nothing wrong with the teacher.

It was obvious that the ESOL personnel will have to come to terms with such cultural or religious issues. It was interesting for us to note that some centres advertised exclusive classes for women. These centres also tried to have only female teachers. There were several issues such as that of health and motherhood that women, particularly those from Asia, liked to discuss only with women. The Huddersfield ESOL centre, for example, advertised 'English courses for women'. These courses were meant for housewives and arranged for classes even at the homes of the learners. Their primary objective was to teach spoken English to help women make their appointments, deal with callers at the door, go shopping, etc. An ESOL teacher remarked: 'There are a variety of pressures that force women to come to ESOL classes.... They have to adjust to the new domestic environment. Secondly, it is just pleasing for them to embark on English, given their problems of isolation, alienation and lack of confidence.'

Syllabus, Materials and Teaching Strategies

Most teachers strongly felt that the curriculum, syllabus, methods and materials to be used would vary from situation to situation. Some ESOL professionals strongly felt that it would not be a good idea to have a national ESOL curriculum as it would strike at the very basis of the spirit of the ESOL programme. At one time, Basic Skills Agency's proposals regarding word-power attracted a lot of attention, but as one ESOL professional said: 'They were so prescriptive and limiting that tutors felt that their hands were tied. I lost patience with it when they tried to apply it to ESOL. It was not about the oral skills; it was not about the ESOL students; and yet it was one certification which was attracting funding.'

Most ESOL teachers felt that though they could benefit from EFL and ESL materials and methods, the needs and situation of ESOL learners made it imperative that innovative methods and materials relevant to the lives of ESOL learners be tried. For example, most EFL materials despite their being well-produced and structurally organised contained topics that were culturally unsuitable for the ESOL learners. For example, it was felt that gender was an important variable: the needs of male and female learners often differed significantly. Many women learners wished to learn English not simply to equip themselves for any specific jobs but to enable them to cope adequately with day-to-day encounters in general and the educational needs of their children in particular. On the other hand, all male learners joined the ESOL centres to improve their employment opportunities. In keeping with these needs in mind, some teachers had made significant innovations in their syllabus and materials. They tried to determine the needs of their learners through informal talks and questionnaires. Most teachers believed that ESOL courses should have a flexible design and should serve as a framework rather than as a rigid straitjacket. One of them said:

> The syllabus is not rigid syllabus.... We devise a syllabus with the students. So in the beginning of the year we talk to the students and discuss what their needs are, what they are hoping to learn, and that goes into the syllabus. In the beginning, the students find that very strange.

Another teacher remarked in a similar vein:

> Their needs are studied very carefully, and then we evolve a syllabus depending on these needs. You cannot evolve one syllabus for all of them because I don't think the needs are all the same for different students. Although there are some common denominators, I don't think that constitutes the core of the syllabus.... Each year we have different students in each class and the syllabus is continually revised.

It is understandable that many of the ESOL learners who came to England without any educational experience, or at best had a hierarchically organised formal educational background, failed to appreciate the 'negotiation approach' to syllabus design and teaching methods. An ESOL teacher recounted a learner's response as follows: 'You are a teacher. You know best. We come here to learn. So you should decide how and what we should learn.'

There was near unanimous agreement among ESOL teachers that there was a need to evolve an indigenous reader, adapt existing materials and produce them on a commercially viable base. These materials should focus, among other things, on such themes as health, shopping, greetings, interview situations, etc. A teacher commented:

> We have got a lot of materials which are often provided for us at the centre. There are various kinds of packs, for example, health packs, social security packs, etc. I would choose a pack that is relevant for my students at a given point of time.

The multilingual and multicultural background of ESOL learners imposes its own constraints on syllabus and methodology. There is generally a considerable variation in terms of their age, sex, socioeconomic background, linguistic skills and cognitive abilities. A teacher said:

> Teaching a group with several mother tongues forces us to change our methods of teaching. We are far more flexible in our methodology now. We use a lot of visuals, activities leading to role-play, trying in the process to teach vocabulary and new structures. They must understand what is going on.

Many teachers felt that Asian women in particular were shy and avoided participating in role-play, etc. in the presence of males. Further, strategies such as mime and mimicry, gestures and role-play, etc. which may be used effectively in the case of children may not work with adults. Adults approach the task of language learning with advanced levels of cognitive and intellectual maturity and may show greater interest in participating in problem-solving activities.

Students' Evaluation

The system of students' learning evaluation was in a state of flux. Very few students took the RSA profile certificate. There were no shorter versions of RSA, nor were there any alternative formal measures of ESOL evaluation. Many teachers felt that evaluation need not be structured: it should be done informally in terms of the communicative tasks a learner was likely to be involved in. One teacher pointed out:

> So everyday, in the beginning of a lesson we fill in a record of work. We look at what we did yesterday and how that relates to the objective. They

also keep a record of this. They keep assessing themselves and when they feel they have learnt the skill they say, 'Well I can do that objective better now than I could do it before. What can I do now?'

Another teacher commented: 'We have a ticking book. When they finish one book then they go and tick the form.... We know how many ticks they should have before they pass and are promoted to the next class.'

Still another said: 'We don't have a syllabus. But we have a list of topics to cover over a period of one year, such as personal identification, coping with certain situations such as at the doctor's surgery.'

In general, most of the teachers said that they opted for an informal evaluation rather than a rigorous assessment or examination. For example, one of the ESOL teachers said:

> We have no formal tests like 'sit-down, do this test', get marks out of a hundred. That I don't do. Obviously, when a student arrives you assess by talking to that student what he or she can do and what the previous learning experience has been. Students also assess themselves since they work along RSA objectives. They each have a copy of the objectives and three times during a year we work together to assess their work.... They are finally given an RSA profile certificate. When they move from one place to another, they carry the records of their work with them.

Teacher Training

There was a general agreement among ESOL teachers that ESOL teaching has not been as professional as it should be. For example, one of the ESOL teachers said: 'A language provision ought to be taken seriously. We must employ trained practitioners. The centre should be supported by libraries, trained personnel and a resource centre.'

In fact, many ESOL teachers were their own informal language learning theorists. They had not received any formal training in ESOL methodology. The number of qualified and trained ESOL teachers was not commensurate with the number of learners. Many of them had EFL training, background and experience. Others were either retired men or part-time mothers. The general principle seemed to be 'if you can speak English well, you can be an ESOL teacher'. Many native and non-native teachers often did not share any language of the ESOL learners. One ESOL teacher remarked: 'There are about 16 languages in a class and I could not speak all the languages, anyway. So I would always have a feeling of being handicapped.... But I encouraged students to help each other using their mother tongues.'

The importance of training teachers in handling multilingual and multicultural classrooms was underscored by one of the ESOL teachers who remarked: 'We have a sort of cultural thing going in the class where we will learn about each other's culture, and certainly I don't think they have come here to learn about the British culture.'

The role of the teacher in teaching a new language has attracted considerable attention during the last few decades. In all the new approaches to second language acquisition, such as the Monitor Model, the Acculturation Model, the Silent Way, Suggestopaedia, etc., there has been increasing emphasis on focusing on the role of the teacher as a facilitator in creating communicative opportunities rather than dominating the learning process. In a multilingual context such as that of ESOL it is particularly important that the learners are allowed to play a more active role than usual. One of the ESOL teachers said: 'I don't generally want to use my mother tongue in the ESOL class but sometimes when they are struggling or they are not clear about something, a word in the mother tongue is very helpful – in English you have to explain a lot but in the mother tongue it is clear and students can often ask each other.'

Future of ESOL

The future of ESOL teaching depends on whether it receives from the authorities all that is due to a mainstream academic and social programme and whether authorities are prepared to increasingly become sensitive to the multilingual and multicultural background of their pupils who are now perceived as clients. This would inevitably involve greater investment of funds, professionalisation of ESOL and our insistence on attendance in the class. As Europe continues to shrink, ESOL is likely to become a more and more powerful movement. If it hopes to meet the challenges of the future, it should become a serious mainstream activity, less anti-racist, more sensitive to multilinguality and have better infrastructure facilities. As the implications of the European Common Market and the increasingly shrinking world manifest themselves, the need for a more radical approach to ESOL will assert itself more emphatically than ever before. We will need to evolve English language teaching syllabi and teaching methodologies that are not isolated from the complexities and compulsions of a day-to-day multilingual and multicultural way of life. The fact that ESOL Centres have now been made a part of Further and Higher Education under the aegis of FEFC is a welcome step towards mainstreaming ESOL. As an experienced ESOL practitioner said:

> This is a step in the right direction because it will not only raise the status of the ESOL learners and teachers but it will also provide library, computer, CD-Rom, etc. facilities to those who wish to use them. Moreover, the future

recruitment will hopefully bring trained language teachers as ESOL tutors. Accountability of both students and teachers will also increase.

Several ESOL professionals expressed their fears about some of the possible consequences of the takeover of the ESOL programme by the FEFC. They wondered whether the flexibility and sensitivity to local needs typically associated with the internal profiles of the erstwhile adult education centres running the ESOL classes may be lost in the demands made by the FEFC. ESOL learners with extremely marginal English language skills may suffer if the demands made by the FEFC are over-ambitious.

Postscript

A recent research project funded by the Basic Skills Agency (which was called ALBSU earlier on) produced a report on ESOL in England, *Lost Opportunities*. They concluded that there is an enormous unmet need for ESOL provision to help the non-English speaking adults to develop their basic skills in English. The Agency organised a seminar in Leeds on 11 March 1997 to disseminate their findings. An ESOL teacher's reaction epitomises the frustrations of those discussed earlier and which continue to be shared by many today:

> We do need good training and staff development for ESOL tutors but it angers me that they can tell us this while only offering the City and Guilds 9285 course, which in my opinion *doesn't* help ESOL tutors do a better job. Given that they have the funds to organise meetings in the Leeds Hilton, where there are facilities and food none of our colleagues or NATECLA could afford, I'd like them to start using that money to organise sessions where ESOL practitioners can get together, exchange ideas and really develop – the sort of thing that NATECLA struggles to do with very little money and no paid workers. (Carter, 1997: 1)

7 Conclusions

Introduction

The underlying primary goal of ESOL teaching throughout its history has been assimilationist in its orientation and the changing ethos has hardly altered it. Not only has the English language establishment used it to dominate, undermine and assimilate the linguistic-cultural communities they have come in close contact with, it has also proved to be much more subtle and effective than the weapons which won the trading ports and colonies in the first place; for even though these are now gone it continues to sustain the British hegemony. It may be noted that the Home Office grant of Section XI funding was an official endorsement of the ESOL field as well as mainstream teachers' growing perception of the multilingual and multicultural composition of their classes, both at schools and at institutions of non-higher tertiary education, especially in the inner city areas of Britain, and of the urgent need to help these ethnic minority pupils/students acquire English language skills to enable them to benefit from education/training and participate as members of the local community; and that both Bullock's Report (DES, 1975) and Swan's Report (DES, 1985) have come to substantially similar assessment, though with different degrees of explicitness and emphasis. Nevertheless, the educational establishment's recognition of the socioeconomically disadvantaged position of the immigrants or of their multilingual/multicultural backgrounds has been no more than mere tokenism and little effort has been made to draw upon what they had already acquired in and through their language and culture in designing and delivering the curriculum, including the ESOL one, to facilitate and accelerate their education and training in the racial hierarchy. Black languages and cultures are thus acknowledged only condescendingly, out of a sense of charity. As Mukherjee points out:

> ESL has become the political aim of standard English. What happens is that by comparison and contrast with the white norm, on the one hand, our people, our cultures and our languages, emerge as abnormal, in need of correction and whitization, and, on the other in the eyes of the elite, our ethnicity and our languages are seen as a function/resource to gain and maintain power. The process affects behaviour, stifles and cripples mental

development and our people are anaesthetized to accept and internalize the coded message of powerlessness contained in the ESL package. (Mukherjee, 1986: 6)

Main Findings

This study has provided empirical support for Gardner & Lambert's (1972) hypothesis that the role of social psychological variables, e.g. attitudes and motivation, in second language proficiency will vary from setting to setting. When a second language is learnt in a non-native context, such as that of learning English in India, Africa, Sri Lanka, etc. social variables seem to be far more important than social-psychological variables. However, when it is learnt in the native settings, e.g. learning English in the UK, social-psychological variables also acquire significance in addition to social variables. In our sample, for example, ESOL learners, who had positive stereotypes of the English language and English people and who had strong integrative motivation as well, were assessed by their teachers to be achieving much higher than those who lacked these attributes. But our detailed analysis clearly shows that language proficiency is not just a matter of motivation and learner's social and linguistic stereotypes; while both the Indian and Pakistani learners had positive social and linguistic stereotypes, their assessed proficiency levels in English are seen to be significantly different. The differences in the proficiency levels could be accounted for in terms of the age at arrival – the mean age of arrival in the case of the Pakistanis was much lower than that of the Indians.

From the interviews with the ESOL teachers it became clear that in spite of the recent changes in the status of ESOL, it may not be able to grow out of its predominantly assimilationist thrust. The integration of the ESOL centres with Higher Education Colleges recently under the aegis of the FEFC may be the beginning of the mainstreaming of the ESOL teaching as a subject/discipline. For more effective and meaningful changes we need to make the ESOL programme more sensitive to the socioeconomic, cultural and linguistic backgrounds of the ESOL learners. Each ESOL centre should, in fact, become an agency for sociopolitical change, and should influence other departments/subject tutors in this understanding of equal opportunities ethos and 'language awareness' in the classroom.

Pedagogical Implications

This study has some very important pedagogical implications for the providers, teachers and teacher trainers, curriculum planners and material producers. It should be the providers' primary objective to make ESOL a mainstream activity and to create enough infrastructure facilities to encourage and facilitate immigrants access to the ESOL centres as early as possible. The teacher-training packages, materials and methodologies should be designed in such a way that they foster positive attitude towards English and the English people without any disrespect for the languages and cultures of ESOL learners. Even an inkling of racism or class and colour discrimination in the classroom could do great damage to the learning process, as it has in the past affected the working classes in the UK and the non-whites in the USA. It seems that learners welcome bilingual teachers in the initial stages though as they progress in their work, they would like the native speakers of English to step in although these native speakers must be sensitive to the sociolinguistic variability existing among the learners. This does not, however, suggest that experienced bilingual tutors are not successful in the advanced classes. Finally, methods and materials should not be divorced from the socioeconomic reality of the learners. The overwhelming support for bilingual methods and materials came from an HMI's report (DES, 1992). It suggested that the use of bilingual tutors and bilingual classroom strategies will significantly enhance the learning process and that bilingual adults achieve success not when they are forced to learn only the language of the host society but when they are offered a wide range of opportunities to use their own languages as well. That the ESOL programme should be aimed at empowerment and should be learner oriented rather than assimilationist is most emphatically brought out by the fact that though immigrants have a very strong desire to learn English their motivations are essentially instrumental and their attitude to English people moderately positive. As reported in the Scottish Further Education Unit (SFEU) 1994 document, Current Issues of Policy and Practice in ESOL, the desire to use English for making friends and leisure time activity has significantly fallen, whereas the percentage of people learning English for employment has increased. It is clear that the future agenda for ESOL teaching should build on the existing languages and values of immigrants and provide them wide and comprehensive educational opportunities. The Basic Skills Agency's remit to promote the improvement of basic skills in English and Welsh only needs to be more flexible and be democratic in its bilingual-orientation. Despite decades of ESOL teaching by dedicated teachers the situation continues to be less than satisfactory. In the report, *Lost Opportunities* (1996) Roy Carr-Hill *et al.* found that three-quarters of their sample of speakers of other languages didn't have 'survival level' ESOL skills and that about one in four failed to attempt the simplest tasks in their 'battery of tests'.

In this later half of the 1990s approaching the new millennium, ESOL has become more insecure as a result of the predominance of the philosophy of the 'market forces' guiding and shaping the educational policies of the government. In this context, Rosenburg (1995) warned that the national targets and levels as satisfactory evidence of performance do not always provide an adequate measure of the achievement of bilingual learners, particularly of early stage learners. What may constitute good teaching and learning for monolingual learners, who appear to be the prime concern of the education system, may be totally inadequate for the bilingual learners, particularly in a migrant context. Rosenburg said:

> The unthinking adoption of these outcome measures, and the assessment of quality against them, can do a considerable disservice to the learners, undermine good teaching and learning and place colleges which make provision for bi-lingual learners at a disadvantage. (Rosenburg, 1995: 27)

In his keynote speech on Managing Change at the NATECLA national conference 1995, Tom Jupp said:

> ... we are constantly being urged to take bold, decisive, one-step action, when it is clear that a canyon cannot be jumped in two steps. However, the metaphor is so striking, and even convincing, that we feel we have nothing left to argue with from the other side.... As economic systems change, there is enormous demand for efficiency and cost reduction, and there is continuous pressure for innovation.... *There is both anger at the inequity of the current situation and a feeling of powerlessness in the midst of it.* (Our emphasis) (Jupp, 1995: 1, 2)

The need for a national strategy for ESOL teaching which recognises the sociolinguistic and pedagogic value of the development of skills in both mother tongue and English is paramount. The rights of the bilingual learners to have the opportunity to develop these skills and the rights of the teachers to have their professionalism recognised and supported no one should deny. There has been inevitable tension between monolingual and bilingual approaches to ESOL, but recent researches in the fields of second language acquisition and bilingualism, and teachers' and learners' own experiences suggest that the way forward is to move ahead on the road to multilingualism and multiculturism.

Appendix I   Questionnaire

Name (optional) ....

1. Sex   Male ☐   Female ☐

2. Age .... 3. Religion .... 4. Occupation ....

5. Were you born in the UK ☐   or   Overseas ☐   ?

6. If born overseas, at what age did you come to the UK? ....

7. Please list the places you have lived in:

		Years	
Name of the country	Name of the town/village	From	to

8. Family background

Relationship to you	Age	Education	Occupation
Father			
Mother			
Husband			
Wife			
Son			
Daughter			
Grandchildren			

9. Schooling

	Country	Medium of instruction	Other languages learnt
Primary			
Middle			
Secondary 'O' level			
Secondary 'A' level			
Any other			

10. Rating of your parents' English skills.
    Indicate by putting a tick (✓) in the appropriate place:

	Skills															
	Understand				Speak				Read				Write			
	not at all	not very well	fairly well	very well	not at all	not very well	fairly well	very well	not at all	not very well	fairly well	very well	not at all	not very well	fairly well	very well
Father																
Mother																	

11. What language/languages did you first speak as a child?

    ....

12. What other languages do you know?

    ....

13. Indicate in the table given below how much you know of each of these languages by putting a tick (✓) in the appropriate place:

	Skills															
	Understand				Speak				Read				Write			
	not at all	not very well	fairly well	very well	not at all	not very well	fairly well	very well	not at all	not very well	fairly well	very well	not at all	not very well	fairly well	very well
1. Mother tongue																
2.																
3.																
4.																

14. Where did you learn English?

In the country of you birth
- (a) at home ☐
- (b) at school ☐
- (c) at work ☐
- (d) from a private tutor ☐
- (e) through friends & relatives ☐
- (f) elsewhere ☐
  (please mention where)

  ....

Outside the country of your birth
- (a) at home ☐
- (b) at school ☐
- (c) at adult education class ☐
- (d) elsewhere ☐
  (please mention where)

  ....

15. Which language/languages do you speak at home?
Indicate by putting a (✓) how often you use each of these languages:

Languages	Every day	Sometimes
1.		
2.		
3.		
4.		

16. Which languages do you generally use at home while talking to the following?

    (a) your wife/husband ....

    (b) parents ....

    (c) grandparents ....

    (d) brothers ....

    (e) sisters ....

    (f) children below 5 years ....

    (g) children older than 5 ....

17. Which languages do you generally use in the following situations?

    (a) talking to relatives who
        do not live with you ....

    (b) talking to your friends
        and neighbours ....

    (c) writing personal letters
        to friends ....

    (d) writing personal letters
        to family/relatives ....

    (e) at places of religious
        worship ....

    (f) at the doctor's ....

    (g) shopping ....

18. Do you have difficulties with English in any of the following?

		Yes	No
(a) talking to:			
	(i) the doctor	☐	☐
	(ii) child's teacher	☐	☐
	(iii) government officials	☐	☐
	(iv) shop assistants	☐	☐
	(v) employees of public transport or other services	☐	☐
(b) Understanding what the doctor says to you		☐	☐
(c) Understanding programmes on TV		☐	☐

	Yes	No
(d) Reading the instructions on the medicines you get	☐	☐
(e) Reading official letters or documents	☐	☐
(f) Reading newspapers and magazines	☐	☐
(g) Any other situation (please say which)	☐	☐

    ....

19. How often to you listen to or watch programmes in English on the radio or TV? Indicate by putting a tick (✓) in the appropriate box.

	Never	Sometimes	Often
Radio			
TV			

20. How often do you listen to or watch programmes in any other language? Indicate by putting a tick (✓) in the appropriate box.

Language	TV			Radio		
	Never	Sometimes	Often	Never	Sometimes	Often

21. Which languages do you mainly use at work?

    (a) with your workmates   ....

    (b) with your boss   ....

    (c) with members of the public ....

22. Do you want to improve your knowledge of English, or your children's?

    Yes ☐   No ☐

    If yes, indicate by putting a tick (✓) how important each skill is for you:

	Most important	Important	Not at all important
Understanding			
Speaking			
Reading			
Writing			

23. Do you want to improve the knowledge of your home language?

        Yes ☐   No ☐

If *yes*, indicate by putting a tick (✓) which skill you would like to acquire:

Understanding ☐   Speaking ☐   Reading ☐   Writing ☐

24. Are your children attending classes in the home language outside school?

        Yes ☐   No ☐

25. Would you like schools to provide lessons in your home language for your children?

        Yes ☐   No ☐

26. Indicate by putting a tick (✓) at the appropriate place your impressions about the English language.

	Very much	*A little*	*Not at all*
Sweet			
Scientific			
Uncivilised			
Useful			
Difficult			

Please answer the following items by ticking (✓) the alternative which appears most applicable to you.

27. During my English lesson I would like

    (a) both my mother tongue and English to be used   ☐

    (b) to have as much mother tongue used as possible   ☐

    (c) to have only English   ☐

28. Whenever I have the opportunity to speak English outside of school, I

    (a) never speak it   ☐

    (b) speak English most of the time   ☐

    (c) speak it occasionally   ☐

29. I find studying English

    (a) not interesting at all   ☐

    (b) no more interesting than other subjects   ☐

    (c) very interesting   ☐

30. When I am in an English class, I
    (a) try to answer as many questions as possible ☐
    (b) answer only the easier questions ☐
    (c) never answer any questions ☐

31. If my teacher wanted us to do an extra English assignment, I would
    (a) offer myself immediately ☐
    (b) offer myself only if the English teacher asked me directly ☐
    (c) not offer myself at all ☐

32. Whenever I have difficulties in the English class I ask the teacher for help
    (a) always ☐
    (b) sometimes ☐
    (c) never ☐

33. Listed below are some of the reasons people may have for learning English as a second language. Please indicate by placing a tick (✓) in the appropriate column how important each reason is for you personally.

Reasons	Very important	Important	Not at all important
(a) To understand better the English-speaking people and their way of life.			
(b) To become independent.			
(c) To gain good friends more easily among English-speaking people.			
(d) To go into business.			
(e) To meet and interact with English-speaking people.			
(f) To think and behave as the English do.			
(g) To get a good job.			
(h) To get quick promotion in my job.			
(i) To acquire qualifications.			
(j) To study English literature.			
(k) Any other reason (please mention).			

34. Below is a list of words that can be used to describe people (for example, hard working, helpful). Put a tick (✓) in the appropriate box to show how well the following words describe THE ENGLISH PEOPLE.

		Very well	A little	Not at all
(1)	hardworking			
(2)	helpful			
(3)	confident			
(4)	pessimistic			
(5)	stubborn			
(6)	unkind			
(7)	foolish			
(8)	efficient			
(9)	nervous			
(10)	cunning			
(11)	successful			
(12)	friendly			
(13)	honest			
(14)	dependable			
(15)	educated			
(16)	shy			

35. Below is a list of words that can be used to describe people (for example, hard working, helpful). Put a tick (✓) in the appropriate box to show how well the following words describe YOUR OWN LINGUISTIC COMMUNITY.

		Very well	A little	Not at all
(1)	hardworking			
(2)	helpful			
(3)	confident			
(4)	pessimistic			
(5)	stubborn			
(6)	unkind			
(7)	foolish			
(8)	efficient			
(9)	nervous			
(10)	cunning			
(11)	successful			
(12)	friendly			
(13)	honest			
(14)	dependable			
(15)	educated			
(16)	shy			

36. Below is a list of words that can be used to describe people (for example, hard working, helpful). Put a tick (✓) in the appropriate box to show how well the following words describe THE WAY YOU WOULD LIKE TO BE.

		Very well	A little	Not at all
(1)	hardworking			
(2)	helpful			
(3)	confident			
(4)	pessimistic			
(5)	stubborn			
(6)	unkind			
(7)	foolish			
(8)	efficient			
(9)	nervous			
(10)	cunning			
(11)	successful			
(12)	friendly			
(13)	honest			
(14)	dependable			
(15)	educated			
(16)	shy			

Appendix II   Rating Sheet

(For Tutors Only)

Name of the student ....

Please indicate in the table given below your evaluation of the English skills of
the student mentioned above:

Skills															
Understand				Speak				Read				Write			
not at all	not very well	fairly well	very well	not at all	not very well	fairly well	very well	not at all	not very well	fairly well	very well	not at all	not very well	fairly well	very well

Any other comment:

Appendix III
ESOL Centre Profile Sheet

Name of the centre: ....

Location: ....

How many teachers does the ESOL centre have? ....

Fees charged from each student: ....

Days on which classes are held, and their timings:

	Mon.	*Tues.*	*Weds.*	*Thurs.*	*Fri.*
Morning					
Evening					

Duration of each class: ....

No. of students in each class: ....

Language-wise distribution of the students:

Language   *No. of students*

....

....

....

....

....

No. of males and females in each class: Males ....   Females ....

No. of students required for starting an ESOL class: ....

No. of students required for continuing an ESOL class: ....

Bibliography

Adorno, T. W., Frenkel-Brunswick, E., Levinson, D. J. and Sanford, R. N. (1950) *The Authoritarian Personality*. New York: Harper.

Agnihotri, R. K. (1979) Processes of assimilation: Sociolinguistic study of Sikh children in Leeds. Unpublished DPhil thesis, University of York.

Agnihotri, R. K. (1987) *Crisis of Identity: The Sikhs in England*. New Delhi: Bahri Publications.

Agnihotri, R. K. (1995) Multilingualism as a classroom resource. In K. Heugh, A. Sieruhn and P. Pluddmann (eds) *Multilingual Education for South Africa* (pp. 3–7). Johannesburgh: Heinemann.

Agnihotri, R. K., Khanna, A. L. and Mukherjee, A. (1984) Use of articles in Indian English: Errors and pedagogical implications. *IRAL* 22(2), 115–9.

Agnihotri, R. K., Khanna, A. L. and Mukherjee, A. (1983) *Variations in the Use of Tenses in English: A Sociolinguistic Perspective* (A report of the ICSSR project). New Delhi: ICSSR.

Agnihotri, R. K., Khanna, A. L. and Mukherjee, A. (1988) *Tense in Indian English*. New Delhi: ICSSR and Bahri Publications.

Aickin, J. (1693) *The English Grammar: Or, the English Tongue Reduced to Grammatical Rules*. London: Printed for the author (Scolar Press 21, 1967).

Aitken, A. J. (1981) The good old Scots tongue: Does Scots have an identity? In E. Haugen *et al.* (eds) *Minority Languages Today* (pp. 7–90). Cambridge: Cambridge University Press.

Allport, G. W. (1954) *The Nature of Prejudice*. Reading, MA: Addison-Wesley.

Anisfeld, E. and Lambert, W. E. (1961) Social and psychological variables in learning Hebrew. *Journal of Abnormal and Social Psychology* 63, 524–9.

Asher, J. J. and Price, B. S. (1967) The learning strategy of the total physical response: Some age differences. *Child Development* 38, 1219–27.

Austin, J. L. (1962) *How to do Things with Words*. Oxford: Oxford University Press.

Banarse, K. (1984) A noise in my ears … and squibbles. In R. Grant and E. Self (eds) *Can You Speak English?* (pp. 58–60). London: Neighbourhood English Classes.

Bartz, W. H. (1974) A study of the relationship of certain learner factors with the ability to communicate in a second language (German for the development of measures of communicative competence). PhD dissertation, Ohio State University.

Bell, R. (1981) *An Introduction to Applied Linguistics*. London: Batsford Academic Press.

Bellin, W. (1984) Welsh and English in Wales. In P. Trudgill (ed.) *Language in the British Isles* (pp. 449–79). Cambridge: Cambridge University Press.

Bhanot, R. and Alibhai, Y. (1988) Issues of anti-racism and equal opportunities in ESL. In S. Nicholls, and E. Hoadley-Maidment (eds) *Current Issues in Teaching English as a Second Language to Adults* (pp. 29–33). Edward Arnold: London.

Bishop, H. (1990) Contradictions in provision for 15–19 (Part II). *Language Issues* 4(1).

Bloomfield, L. (1926) A set of postulates for the science of language. *Language* 2, 153–64.

105

Brown, H. D. (1972) Cognitive pruning and second language acquisition. *Modern Language Journal* 56, 218–22.

Brown, H. D. (1973) Affective variables in second language acquisition. *Language Learning* 23, 231–44.

Burstall, C. (1975) Factors affecting foreign language learning: A consideration of some recent research findings. *Language Teaching and Linguistics: Abstracts* 8(1), 5–21.

Burstall, C., Jamieson, M., Cohen, S. and Hargreaves, M. (1974) *Primary French in the Balance*. Slough: NFER.

Burt, M. and Dulay, H. (1980) On acquisition orders. In S. Felix (ed.) *Second Language Development: Trends and Issues*. Tubingen: Gunter Narr.

Buteau, M. F. (1970) Students' errors and learning of French as a second language: Pilot study. *IRAL* 8(2), 133–45.

Cameron, D. *et al.* (1992) *Researching Language: Issues of Power and Method*. London: Routledge.

Candlin, C. N., Leather, J. and Bruton, C. (1974) English language skills for overseas doctors and medical staff. *Work in Progress I–IV.* Mimeo, University of Lancaster.

Carr-Hill, R., Passingham, S., Wolf, A. with Kent, N. (1996) *Lost Opportunities: The Language Skills of Linguistic Minorities in England and Wales*. The Basic Skills Agency.

Carroll, J. B. (1962) The prediction of success in intensive foreign language training. In G. Robert (ed.) *Training Research and Education* (pp. 86–136). Pittsburgh: University of Pittsburgh.

Carroll, J. B. (1963a) A model of school learning. *Teachers College Record* 64, 723–33.

Carroll, J. B. (1963b) Research on teaching foreign languages. In N. L. Gage (ed.) *Handbook of Research on Teaching*. Chicago: Rand McNally.

Carroll, J. B. (1966) The contributions of psychological theory and educational research to the teaching of foreign languages. In A. Valdman (ed.) *Trends in Language Teaching*. New York: McGraw-Hill.

Carroll, J. B. and Sapon, S. M. (1959) *Modern Language Aptitude Test, MLAT Manual*. New York: The Psychological Corporation.

Carter, L. (1997) Cause for concern. Basic Skills Agency report on seminar. In *NATECLA News*, No. 53, Summer 1997.

Cheshire, J. (1991) The UK and the USA. In J. Cheshire (ed.) *English Around the World*. Cambridge: Cambridge University Press.

Chomsky, N. (1957) *Syntactic Structures*. The Hague: Mouton.

Chomsky, N. (1959) Review of Skinner's verbal behaviour. *Language* 35, 26–58.

Chomsky, N. (1965) *Aspects of the Theory of Syntax*. Cambridge: MIT Press.

Chomsky, N. (1966) The utility of linguistic theory to the language teacher. In J. P. B. Allen and S. P. Corder (eds) (1973) *Readings for Applied Linguistics* (pp. 234–40). Oxford: Oxford University Press (the Edinburgh Course in Applied Linguistics Vol. I).

Chomsky, N. (1968) *Language and Mind*. New York.

Chomsky, N. (1988) *Language and Problems of Knowledge: The Managua Lectures*. Cambridge, MA: MIT Press.

Clahsen, H. (1980) Psycholinguistic aspects of L2-acquisition: Word order phenomena in foreign workers' interlanguage. In S. Felix (ed.) *Second Language Development: Trends and Issues* (pp. 57–79). Tubingen: Gunter Narr.

Clahsen, H. and Muysken, P. (1986) The availability of universal grammar to child and adult learners. *Second Language Research* 2, 93–119.

Clyne, M. (1968) Zum Pidgin-Deutsch der Gastarbeiter. *Zeitschrift für Mundart-forschung* 35, 130–9. (Cited from Perdue, 1984).

Cook, V. J. (1978) Second language learning: A psycholinguistic perspective (survey article). *Language Teaching Abstracts* 11(2), 73–84.

Cook, V. J. (1991) *Second Language Learning and Language Teaching*. London: Edward Arnold.

Corder, S. P. (1967) The significance of learners' errors. *IRAL* 5(4), 161–70.

Corder, S. P. (1971) Idiosyncratic dialects and error analysis. *IRAL* 9(2), 147–59.

Corder, S. P. (1973) *Introducing Applied Linguistics*. Harmondsworth: Penguin.

Corder, S. P. (1974) The elicitation of interlanguage. *IRAL* (pp. 51–63). Special issue on the occasion of B. Malmberg's 60th birthday, G. Nickel (ed.).

Department of Education and Science (DES) (1975) *A Language for Life. 'The Bullock Report'*. London: HMSO.

Department of Education and Science (DES) (1985) *Education for All (The Swann Report)*. London: HMSO.

Department of Education and Science (DES) (1992) *Bilingual Adults in Education and Training*. London: HMSO.

Dickerson, L. J. (1974) Internal and external patterning of phonological variability in the speech of Japanese learners of English: Towards a theory of second language acquisition. PhD dissertation, University of Illinois, Urbana-Champaign.

Dorian, N. (1981) *Language Death: The Life Cycle of a Scottish Gaelic Dialect*. Chicago: University of Pennsylvania Press.

Douglas, J. W. B. (1964) *The Home and the School: A Study of Ability and Attainment in the Primary School*. London: MacGibbon & Kee.

Dulay, H. and Burt, M. (1974) Natural sequences in child second language acquisition. *Language Learning* 24, 37–53.

Dulay, H. and Burt, M. (1975) A new approach to discovering universal strategies of child second language acquisition. In D. Dato (ed.) *Developmental Psycholinguistics: Theory and Applications* (Georgetown University Linguistics) (pp. 209–33). Washington: Georgetown University Press.

Dulay, H. and Burt, M. (1977) Some remarks on creativity in language acquisition. In W. C. Ritchie (ed.) (1978) *Second Language Acquisition Research: Issues and Implications*. New York: Academic Press.

Duskova, L. (1969) On the sources of errors in foreign language learning. *IRAL* 7, 11–36.

Fairclough, N. (1989) *Language and Power*. London: Longman.

Fairclough, N. (ed.) (1992) *Critical Language Awareness*. London: Longman.

Fasold, R. (1984) *The Sociolinguistics of Society*. Oxford: Blackwell.

Feenstra, H. J. and Gardner, R. C. (1968) Aptitude, attitude and motivation in second language acquisition. *Research Bulletin No. 101*, University of Western Ontario.

Felix, S. W. (1981) Some introductory notes concerning contrastive linguistics. In J. Fisiak (ed.) *Contrastive Linguistics and Language Teacher*. Pergamon Institute of English.

Flynn, S. and Espinal, I. (1985) Head-initial/head-final parameter in adult Chinese L2 acquisition of English. *Second Language Research* 1, 93–117.

Fries, C. C. (1945) *Teaching and Learning of English as a Foreign Language*. Ann Arbor: University of Michigan Press.

Fromkin, V., Krashen, S., Curtiss, S., Rigler, D. and Rigler, M. (1974) The development of language in Genie: A case of language acquisition beyond the critical period. *Brain and Language* 1, 81–107.

Furnborough, P., Jupp, T, Munns, R. and Roberts, C. (1982) Language, disadvantage and discrimination: Breaking the cycle of minority group perception. *Journal of Multilingual and Multicultural Development* 3(3), 247–66.

Gardner, R. C. (1966) Motivational variables in second language learning. *International Journal of American Linguistics* 32, 24–44.

Gardner, R. C. (1985) *Social Psychology and Second Language Learning: The Role of Attitudes and Motivation.* London: Edward Arnold.

Gardner, R. C. (1988) The socio-educational model of second language learning: Assumptions findings and issues. *Language Learning* 38(1), 75–94.

Gardner, R. C. and Lambert, W. E. (1959) Motivational variables in second language acquisition. *Canadian Journal of Psychology* 13, 226–72.

Gardner, R. C. and Lambert, W. E. (1965) Language aptitude, intelligence and second language achievement. *Journal of Educational Psychology* 56(4), 191–99.

Gardner, R. C. and Lambert, W. E. (1972) *Attitudes and Motivation in Second Language Learning.* Rowley, MA: Newbury House.

Ghadessey, M. (1980) Implications of error analysis for second/foreign language acquisition. *IRAL* 18(2), 93–104.

Gradman, H. L. (1971) What methodologists ignore in contrastive teaching. Paper presented at the Pacific Conference on Contrastive Linguistics and Language Universals, Honolulu.

Grant, R. and Self, E. (1984) (eds) *Can You Speak English?* London: Neighbourhood English Classes.

Green, P. S. (1977) Aptitude test. *Journal of National Association of Language Advisers* 8.

Grosjean, F. (1982) *Life with Two Languages: An Introduction to Bilingualism.* Cambridge, MA: Harvard University Press.

Gumperz, J. J. (ed.) (1982a) *Discourse Strategies: Studies in Interactional Sociolinguistics 1.* Cambridge: Cambridge University Press.

Gumperz, J. J. (ed.) (1982b) *Language and Social Identity: Studies in Interactional Sociolinguistics 2.* Cambridge: Cambridge University Press.

Gumperz, J. J. and Roberts, C. (1978) *Developing Awareness Skills for Inter-ethnic Communication.* Southall: National Centre for Industrial Language Training.

Gumperz, J. J., Jupp, T. and Roberts, C. (1979) *Crosstalk.* Southall: National Centre for Industrial Language Training.

Gumperz, J. J., Jupp, T. and Roberts, C. (1980) *Crosstalk – The Wider Perspective.* Southall: National Centre for Industrial Language Training.

Guthrie, E . R. (1935) *The Psychology of Learning.* New York: Arbor.

Hallgarten, K. and Hayman, R. (1984) How we began. In R. Grant and E. Self (eds) *Can You Speak English?* (pp. 7–15). London: Neighbourhood English Classes.

Halliday, M. A. K. (1967) *Intonation and Grammar in British English.* The Hague: Mouton.

Halliday, M. A. K. (1975) *Learning How to Mean: Explorations in the Development of Language.* London: Edward Arnold.

Hatch, E. (1976) Conversational analysis: An alternative methodology for second language acquisition research. *Proceedings of the NWAVE-V Conference.* Georgetown, USA.

Howatt, A. (1974) Programmed instruction. In J. P. B. Allen and S. P. Corder (eds) *Techniques in Applied Linguistics (The Edinburgh Course in Applied Linguistics, Vol. 3).*

Howatt, A. P. R. (1984) *A History of English Language Teaching.* Oxford: Oxford University Press.

Hymes, D. (1971) On communicative competence. In J. B. Pride and J. Holmes (eds) (1972) *Sociolinguistics.* Harmondsworth: Penguin.

Hulstijn, J. (1982) *Monitor Use by Adult Second Language Learners.* Meppel: Krips.

Hutchinson, T. and Waters, A. (1987) *English for Specific Purposes: A Learning-centered Approach.* Cambridge: Cambridge University Press.

Hyltenstam, K. (1977) Implicational patterns in interlanguage syntax variation. *Language Learning* 27(2), 388–411.

Jakobovits, L. A. (1970) *Foreign Language Learning: A Psycholinguistic Analysis of the Issues.* Rowley, MA: Newbury House.

Jakobovits, L. A. and Gordon, B. (1974) *The Context of Foreign Language Teaching.* Rowley, MA: Newbury House.

Janks, H. (ed.) (1993) *Critical Language Awareness Series: Materials for the Classroom.* Johannesburg: Hodder & Stoughton.

Jansen, B. and Lalleman, J. (1980a) Interferentie en woordvolgorde, het Nederlands van buytenlandse arbeiders (pp. 1–48). Instiuut algemene Taalwetenschap Amsterdam 27. (Cited from Perdue, 1984).

Jansen, B. and Lalleman, J. (1980b) De invloed van de moedertaal op de zins bouw van het Nederlands van Turkse en Marokkaanse arbeiders. In R. Appel *et al.* (eds) *Taalproblemen van Buitenlandse Arbeiders en hun Kinderen* (pp. 137–50). Coutinho, Muiderberg. (Cited from Perdue, 1984).

Jansen, B., Lalleman, J. and Muysken, P. (1981) The alternation hypothesis: Acquisition of Dutch word order by Turkish and Moroccan foreign workers. *Language Learning* 31(2), 315–36.

Janssen, A. (1992) It's like guerrilla warfare really ... not terribly planned: A study of the education and training opportunities available to bilingual learners in the post 16 sector. MA dissertation, University of London.

Jaworski, A. (1994) Pragmatic failure in a second language: Greeting responses in English by Polish students. *IRAL* 32(1), 41–55.

Jupp, T. (1995) Managing change. NATECLA national conference keynote speech. In *NATECLA News* No. 48, Autumn 1995.

Kagan, J. (1965) Reflexion – impulsivity and reading ability in primary grade children. *Child Development* 36, 609–28.

Kanji, G. (1984) How I became a home tutor organiser. In R. Grant and E. Self (eds) *Can You Speak English?* (pp. 83–4).

Kay, B. (1986) *The Mother Tongue.* Ayrshire, Scotland: Alloway.

Khanna, A. L. (1983) A study of some learner variables in learning English as a second language. PhD thesis, University of Delhi.

Khanna, A. L. and Agnihotri, R. K. (1982) Language achievement and some social psychological variables. *CIEFL Bulletin* 18, 41–51.

Khanna, A. L. and Agnihotri, R. K. (1984) Some predictors of speech skills: A socio-psychological study. *International Journal of Dravidian Lingusitics* 13(2), 229–51.

Khanna, A. L., Verma, M. K., Agnihotri, R. K. and Sinha, S. K. (1990) Attitudes and motivation of adult ESOL learners in Great Britain: A cross-cultural pilot study. *Language Issues* 4(1), 4–8.

Klein. W. (1986) *Second Language Acquisition.* Cambridge: Cambridge University Press.

Kotsinas, U. B. (1980) Kommer och predikatet GO: funderingar kring tempus och aspekt i invandrarsvenska. In Tvåspråkighet, Föridrag från Tredje Nordiska Tvåspråkighet-symposiet, 4–5 Juni, 1980. In E. Ejerhed and I. Henrysson (eds) *Umeå Studies in the Humanities* 36. (Cited from Perdue, 1984).

Krashen, S. D. (1978a) Individual variation in the use of the monitor. In W. C. Ritchie (ed.) *Second Language Acquisition Research: Issues and Implications.* Academic Press.

Krashen, S. D. (1978b) The monitor model for second language acquisition research. In R. C. Gingras (ed.) *Second Language Acquisition and Foreign Language Teaching* (pp. 1–26). Arlington, VA: Center for Applied Linguistics.

Krashen, S. D. (1982) *Principles and Practice in Second Language Acquisition.* Oxford: Pergamon Press.

Krashen, S. D. (1985) *The Input Hypothesis: Issues and Implications.* London: Longman.

Kress, G. and Hodge, R. (1979) *Language as Ideology.* London: Routledge.

Labov, W. (1966) *The Social Stratification of English in New York City.* Washington, DC: The Center for Applied Linguistics.

Labov, W. (1969) Contradiction, deletion and inherent variability of the English copula. *Language 45,* 715–62.

Labov, W. (1972) *Sociolinguistic Patterns.* Oxford: Blackwell.

Lambert, W. E. (1974) Cultural and language factors in learning and education. Paper presented at the Vth Annual Learning Symposium on Cultural Factors in Learning at Western Washington State College, Belingham, Washington.

Lambert, W. E., Gardener, R. C., Barik, H. C. and Tunstall, K. (1962) Attitudinal and cognitive aspects of intensive study of a second language. *Journal of Abnormal and Social Psychology* 66, 358–68.

Larsen-Freeman, D. E. (1976) An explanation for the morpheme acquisition order of second language learners. *Language Learning* 26(1), 125–34.

Lee, W. R. (1968) Thoughts on contrastive linguistics in the context of language teaching. In J. E. Alatis (ed.) *Monograph Series on Language and Linguistics, 21: Contrastive Linguistics and its Pedagogical Implications.* Washington DC: Georgetown University.

Leech, G. and Svartvik, J. (1975) *A Communicative Grammar of English.* London: Longman.

Leino, A. L. (1972) *English School Achievement and Some Students Characteristics I.* Research Bulletin 33. Institute of Education, University of Helsinki, Finland.

Leino, A. L. (1974) *English School Achievement and Some Students Characteristics II.* Research Bulletin 40. Institute of Education, University of Helsinki, Finland.

Lenneberg, E. H. (1967) *The Biological Foundation of Language.* New York: Wiley.

Loveday, L. (1982) *The Sociolinguistics of Learning and Using a Non-native Language.* Oxford: Pergamon Press.

Lukmani, Y. M. (1972) Motivation to learn and language proficiency. *Language Learning* 22(2), 261–73.

Macnamara, J. (1973) Nurseries, streets and classrooms: Some companions and deductions. *Modern Language Journal* 57, 250–4.

Malmberg, B. (1971) Applications of linguistics. In G. E. Perren and J. L. M. Trim (eds) *Applications of Linguistics.* Cambridge: Cambridge University Press.

Maittaire, M. (1712) *The English Grammar: Or an Essay on the Art of Grammar, Applied to and Exemplified in the English Tongue.* London: W.B.

Marton, W. (1981) Pedagogical implications of contrastive analysis. In J. Fisiak (ed.) *Contrastive Linguistics and the Language Teacher.* Pergamon Institute of English.

Mathur, C. (1991) The role of attitudes and motivation in foreign language learning: The case of German in India. M.Phil dissertation, University of Delhi, Delhi.

Mayell, F. L. (1958) English for our coloured citizens. *Adult Education* 30(4), 271–4.

McLaughlin, B. (1990) The relationship between first and second languages: Language proficiency and language aptitude. In B. Harley, P. Allen, T. Cummins and M. Swain (eds) *The Development of Second Language Proficiency* (pp. 158–74). Cambridge: Cambridge University Press.

Mills, V. (1994) Partnership and ESOL. In *Current Issues of Policy and Practice.* SEFU.

Morris, J. M. (1966) *Standards and Progress in Reading.* Slough: NFER.

Morrow, K. (1981) Principles of communicative methodology. In K. Johnson and K. Morrow (eds) *Communication in the Classroom.* London: Longman.

Morse, N. C. and Allport, F. H. (1952) The causation of anti-semitism: An investigation of seven hypotheses. *Journal of Psychology* 34, 197–233.

Morsly, D. (1976) Interferences de l'arabe sur le français des travailleurs immigrés à Paris. University of Paris V, Paris. (Cited from Perdue, 1984).

Morsly, D. and Vasseur, M. T. (1976) L'emploi des verbes français par les travailleurs immigrés arabophones et portugais. *Langue Française* 29, 80–92. (Cited from Perdue, 1984).

Mowrer, O. M. (1954) The psychologist looks at language. *American Psychologist* 9, 660–94.

Mueller, T. H. (1971) Student attitudes in the basic French courses at the University of Kentucky. *Modern Language Journal* 55(5), 290–98.

Mukherjee, A. (1980) Language maintenance and language shift. Thesis, University of Delhi.

Mukherjee, T. (1986) ESL: An imported new empire? *Journal of Moral Education* 15(1), 43–9.

Munby, J. (1978) *Communicative Syllabus Design.* Cambridge: Cambridge University Press.

Naiman, N. *et al.* (1978) *The Good Language Learner.* Toronto: Ontario Institute of Studies in Education.

Nemser, W. (1971a) Problems and prospects in contrastive linguistics. Paper presented at the International Conference on Modern Linguistics and Language Teaching, Hungary, April, 1971.

Nemser, W. (1971b) Approximative systems of foreign language learners. *IRAL* 9(2), 115–23.

Newmark, L. (1966) How not to interfere with language learning. *IJAL* 32(1), 77–83.

Newmark, L. and Reibel, D. A. (1968) Necessity and sufficiency in language learning. *IRAL* 6, 145–64.

Nicholls, S. and Hoadley-Maidment, E. (eds) (1988) *Current Issues in Teaching English as a Second Language to Adults.* London: Edward Arnold.

Nickel, G. and Wagner, K. H. (1968) Contrastive linguistics and language teaching. *IRAL* 6, 233–55.

Nida, E. A. (1958) Some psychological problems in second language learning. *Language Learning* 8(1), 7–15.

Nisbet, J. D. and Welsh, J. (1972) A local evaluation of primary school French. *Journal of Curriculum Studies* 4(2), 169–75.

Oller, J. Jr (1972a) Contrastive analysis, difficulty and predictability. *Foreign Language Annals* 6, 95–106.

Oller, J. Jr (1972b) Scoring methods of difficulty levels for cloze tests of ESL proficiency. *Modern Language Journal* 56, 151–8.

Oller, J. Jr (1976) A programme for language testing research. *Language Learning* (Special Issue) 4, 141–66.

Oller, J. Jr, Hudson, A. J. and Lie, P. F. (1977) Attitudes and attained proficiency in ESL: A socio-linguistic study of native speakers of Chinese in the United States. *Language Learning* 27, 1–26.

Oller, J. Jr and Richards, J. C. (eds) (1983) *Focus on the Learner: Pragmatic Perspectives for the Language Teacher.* Rowley, MA: Newbury House.

Olson, L. L. and Samuels, S. J. (1973) The relationship between age and accuracy of foreign language. *Journal of Educational Research* 66(6), 263–8.

Oppenheim, A. N. (1966) *Questionnaire Design and Attitude Measurement.* London: Heinemann.

Osgood, C. E. (1963) On understanding and creating sentences. *American Psychologist* 18, 735–51.

Osgood, C. E. (1968) Towards a wedding of insufficiencies. In T. R. Dixon and D. L. Horton (eds) *Verbal Behavior and General Behavior Theory.* Englewood Cliffs, NJ: Prentice-Hall.

Pavlov, I. P. (1927) *Conditioned Reflexes* (Translated by G. V. Anrep). London: Oxford University Press.

Peal, E. and Lambert, W. E. (1962) The relation of bilingualism to intelligence. *Psychological Monographs* LXXVI, No. 27 (Whole issue No. 546).

Penfield, W. (1953) A consideration of neuro-physiological mechanisms of speech and some educational consequences. *Proceedings of the American Academy of Arts and Sciences* 82, 201–14.

Perdue, C. (ed.) (1984) *Second Language Acquisition by Adult Immigrants: A Field Manual.* Rowley, MA: Newbury House.

Pichel, L. (1980) Les interférences linguistiques (phonétiques, syntaxiques et culturelles) des Espagnols immigrés en France. University of Paris III, Paris. (Cited from Perdue, 1984).

Pimsleur, P. (1966) *Pimsleur Language Aptitude Battery – Form 5.* New York: Harcourt, Brace & World.

Pimsleur, P., Mosberg, L. and Morrison, A. L. (1962) Student factors in foreign language learning. *Modern Language Journal* 46, 160–70.

Pimsleur, P., Sundland, D. M. and McIntyr, R. D. (1964) Underachievement in foreign language learning. *IRAL* 2, 113–50.

Poole, J. (1646) *The English Accidence: Or, a short, plaine and easie way, for the more speedy attaining to the Latine tongue, by the help of the English.* London: R.C. (Scolar Press 5, 1967).

Prabhu, N. S. (1987) *Second Language Pedagogy.* Oxford: Oxford University Press.

Preston, D. R. (1989) *Sociolinguistics and Second Language Acquisition.* London: Basil Blackwell.

Quirk, R., Greenbaum, S., Leech, G. and Svartvik, J. (1972) *A Grammar of Contemporary English.* London: Longman.

Quirk, R. and Greenbaum, S. (1973) *A University Grammar of English.* London: Longman.

Ramsey, C. A. and Wright, E. N. (1974) Age and second language learning. *Journal of Social Psychology* 94, 51–121.

Reber, A. S. (1973) On psycholinguistic paradigms. *Journal of Psycholinguistic Research* 2(4), 289–319.

Richards, J. C. (1971a) A non-contrastive approach to error analysis. *English Language Teaching* 25, 204–19. Quoted in the text from Richards and Sampson (ed.) 1974 (pp. 172–88).

Richards, J. C. (1971b) Error analysis and second language strategies. *Language Sciences* 17, 12–22.

Richards, J. C. (1972) Social factors, interlanguage and language learning. *Language Learning* 22(2), 159–88.

Richards, J. C. (1973) Error analysis and second language strategies. In J. W. Oller and J. C. Richards (eds).

Richards, J. C. and Sampson, G. P. (1974) The study of learner English, In J. C. Richards (ed.) *Error Analysis: Perspectives on Second Language Acquisition.* London: Longman.

Ritchie, W. C. (1978) *Second Language Acquisition Research: Issues and Implications.* New York: Academic Press.

Rivers, W. (1964) *The Psychologist and the Foreign Language Teacher.* Chicago: University of Chicago Press.

Roberts, J. T. (1975) Recent developments in ELT – Part I and bibliography. *Language Teaching Abstracts* 94–104.

Robinson,W. P. (1971) Social factors and language development in primary school children. In R. Huxley and E. Ingram (eds) *Language Acquisition: Models and Methods*. New York: Academic Press.

Romaine, S. (1982) The English language in Scotland. In R. W. Bailey and M. Gorlach (eds) *English as a World Language* (pp. 56–83). Ann Arbor: University of Michigan Press.

Rosansky, E. J. (1976) Methods and morphemes in second language acquisition research. *Language Learning* 26(2), 409–25.

Rosenburg, S. (1995) Quality assurance and ESOL: Based on the keynote address given at the NATECLA conference, July 1994. In *Language Issues* Vol. 7(1), 1995 (pp. 25–7).

Saifullah Khan, V. (1980) The 'mother-tongue' of linguistic minorities in multi-cultural England. *Journal of Multilingual and Multicultural Development* 1, 71–88.

Sadighi, F. (1994) The acquisition of English restrictive relative clauses by Chinese, Japanese and Korean adult native speakers. *IRAL* 32(2), 141–53.

Sahgal, A. (1983) A sociolinguistic study of the spoken English of Delhi elite. MPhil thesis, University of Delhi.

Santos-Pereira, C. (1981) Problèmes de bilingualisme et interférences chez les travailleurs portugais immigrés en France. University of Paris V, Paris. (Cited from Perdue, 1984).

Satyanath, T. S. (1982) Kannadigas in Delhi: A sociolinguistic study. Unpublished MPhil dissertation, University of Delhi.

Sawhney, C. (1997) Acquisition of Hindi as a second language by Tamils in Delhi: A social psychological perspective. Doctoral thesis submitted to the University of Delhi, Delhi.

Scherer, K. R. and Giles, H. (eds) (1979) *Social Markers in Speech*. Cambridge: Cambridge University Press.

Schumann, J. H. (1978) The acculturation model for second language acquisition. In R. C. Gingras (ed.) *Second Language Acquisition and Foreign Language Teaching* (pp. 27–50). Arlington, VA: Center for Applied Language Teaching.

Searle, J. R. (1969) *Speech Acts*. Cambridge: Cambridge University Press.

Seliger, H. W. (1978) Implications of multiple critical periods hypothesis for second language learning. In W. C. Ritchie (ed.) *Second Language Acquisition Research*. New York: Academic Press.

Selinker, L. (1969) Language transfer. *General Linguistics* 9, 67–92.

Selinker, L. (1972) Interlanguage. *IRAL* 10(3), 219–31.

Sheth, I. (1984) The student. In R. Grant and E. Self (eds) *Can You Speak English?* (pp. 52–7). London: Neighbourhood English Classes.

Singh, R., Lele, J. K. and Martohardjono, G. (1988) Communication in a multilingual society: Some missed opportunities. *Language in Society* 17(1), 43–59.

Skehan, P. (1989) *Individual Differences in Second Language Learning*. London: Edward Arnold.

Skinner, B. F. (1954) The science of learning and the art of teaching. *Harvard Ed. Review* 24, 86–97.

Skinner, B. F. (1957) *Verbal Behaviour*. New York: Appleton-Century Crofts.

Smart, J., Elton, C. F. and Burnett, C. W. (1970) Underachievers and overachievers in intermediate French. *Modern Language Journal* 54(6), 415–20.

Spiers, A. (1992) Interview with Jean McAllister. *NATECLA News*, 39, Spring 12–13, Birmingham.

Spolsky, B. (1966) A psycholinguistic critique of programmed foreign language instruction. *IRAL* 4(2), 119–27.

Sridhar, S. N. (1981) Contrastive analysis, error analysis, and interlanguage: Three phases of one goal. In J. Fisiak (ed.) *Contrastive Linguistics and the Language Teacher.* Oxford: Pergamon .

Srole, L. (1951) Social dysfunction, personality and social distance attitudes. Paper read before The American Sociology Society, National Meeting, Chicago, IL (mimeo).

Stevick, E. (1976) *Memory, Meaning and Method.* Rowley, MA: Newbury House.

Strevens, P. (1968) *Styles of Learning Among American Indians: An Outline for Research.* Washington DC.

Strevens, P. (1969) Two ways of looking at error analysis. *ERIC: ED* 037714. Washington: ERIC.

Strevens, P. (1977) English as an international language: When is a local form of English suitable target for ELT purposes? *ELT Documents.*

Thorpe, F. (1994) Introduction. *Current Issues of Policy and Practice in ESOL.* Scottish Further Education Unit (SFEU).

Titone, R. (1977) Teaching second language in multilingual/multicultural contexts. Paper presented at *UNESCO Meeting in Paris,* 1977 (Dec.).

Tremaine, R. V. (1975) Piagetian equilibration, processes in *syntax learning.* In D. P. Dato (ed.) *Psycholinguistics: Theory and Applications.* Georgetown University Round Table.

Trudgill, P. (1974) *The Social Differentiation of English in Norwich.* London: Cambridge University Press.

TSAS (1991) *A Survey of English for Speakers of Other Languages in Occupational Training.* London: Department of Employment.

Valdman, A. (1970) Toward a better implementation of the audio-lingual approach. *Modern Language Journal* 54(5), 309–19.

Verma, Mahendra K. (1986) From Macaulay to Michael Swann: The language education of South Asian children. Paper presented at XI World Sociological Congress, New Delhi.

Verma, Mahendra K. (1993) Bilingual children, mother tongue, ESL and standard English. Paper presented at the 1993 International Convention on Language in Education: English, Whose English. University of East Anglia, Norwich, UK.

Weigel, M. M. and Weigel, R. M. (1985) Directive use in a migrant agricultural community: A test of Ervin-Tripp's hypotheses. *Language in Society* 14, 63–79.

Weinreich, U. (1953) *Languages in Contact.* The Hague: Mouton.

Whitaker, H. A. (1978) Bilingualism: A neurolinguistics perspective. In W. C. Ritchie (ed.) *Second Language Acquisition Research: Issues and Implications.* New York: Academic Press.

Whitman, R. A. and Jackson, K. L. (1972) The unpredictability of contrastive analysis. *Language Learning* 22, 29–41.

Widdowson, H. G. (1973) Directions in the teaching of discourse. In S. P. Corder and E. Roulet (eds) *Theoretical Linguistics Models in Applied Linguistics.* Brussels: AIMAV/Didiar.

Wilkins, D. A. (1972) Grammatical, situational and notional syllabuses. *Proceedings of the 3rd International Congress of Applied Linguistics.* Heidelberg: Julius Groos Verlag.

Wilkins, D. A. (1974a) A communicative approach to syllabus construction in adult language learning. *Modern Languages in Adult Education.* EES/Symposium 57, 10. Strasbourg: Council of Europe.

Wilkins, D. A. (1974b) Notional syllabuses and the concept of a minimum adequate grammar. In S. P. Corder and E. Roulet (eds) *Linguistic Insights in Applied Linguistics.* Brussels: AIMAV/Didier.

Wilkins, D. A. (1976) *Notional Syllabuses*. Oxford: Oxford University Press.

Williams, D. (1981) Factors related to performance in reading English as a second language. *Language Learning* 31(1), 31–50.

Williams, G. (1992) *Sociolinguistics: A Sociological Critique*. London: Routledge.

Williams, S. H. (1958) English for foreigners: An aspect of liberal studies. *Adult Education* 31(12), 116–24.

Wittenborn, J. R. and Larsen, R. P. (1944) A factorial study of achievement in college German. *Journal of Educational Psychology* 35, 39–48.

Wittenborn, J. R., Larsen, P. R. and Mogil, R. L. (1945) An empirical evaluation of study habits for college course in French and Spanish. *Journal of Educational Psychology* 36(8), 449–74.

WTBW (Werkgroep Taal Buitenlandse Werknemers) (1980) Taalattitude, taalvaardigheid, en sociale omstandigheden van Marokkaanse arbeiders in Nederland: een verkennend onderzoek. In P. Muysken (ed.) *De Verwerving van het Nederlands door Buitenlandse arbeiders* (pp. 49–106). Instituut Algemene Taalwetenschap Amsterdam 27. (Cited from Perdue, 1984).

Index

Authors

Subjects